Lives in Cricket: No 10

John Shepherd

The Loyal Cavalier

Paddy Briggs

With a foreword by Sir Everton Weekes

First published in Great Britain by
Association of Cricket Statisticians and Historians
Cardiff CF11 9XR

British Library Cataloguing-in-Publication Data.
A catalogue record for this book is available from the British Library.

ISBN: 978 1 905138 76 0
Typeset by Limlow Books

Contents

Foreword
by Everton Weekes, KCMG, GCM, OBE

I first met the young John Shepherd when I was the government cricket coach of Barbados in the early 1960s. John was at Alleyne School in St Andrew, which had already produced the great Conrad Hunte, and as soon as I saw him I felt that he too had a special ability. John had a good natural talent but what particularly impressed me was that, although he was a little shy, he was so eager to learn and he listened very carefully to what I said – I was trying to help him in all aspects of the game. I selected John for a schoolboy team that I coached and managed on a short tour to Jamaica in 1961 and he performed very well as a genuine allrounder and he seemed, even as a youngster, to have a good brain for the game.

In 1965 I was working with the Barbados team when there was a tour by the International Cavaliers who were managed by Les Ames and captained by Trevor Bailey – they asked me whether there were any good young Bajan cricketers who might be suitable for county cricket. I recommended John Shepherd and his good friend Keith Boyce and that led to the two of them going to England – John to Kent and Keith to Essex. Before they went I gave them a few tips on how to play and how to behave which I had learned from my time in the Leagues and I know that John listened to me!

John was from the same sort of humble background as me and most of the black cricketers in Barbados and we all had to work hard to progress in the game in those days. I was sure that John had both the attitude and the talent to do well in England and I followed his career there quite closely and was delighted with his success.

When John Shepherd was around twenty I thought that he had the potential to be a Test cricketer – he was a good bowler, a good batsman and a very good fielder and he had a good head for one so young. Unfortunately for him he was around at the same time as some of the truly greats of West Indies cricket – Sobers, Kanhai, Lloyd, Roberts, Richards, Holding and the rest – he couldn't quite cement a place in the team. Had John been a young man today he would have been one of the first names on the West Indies team sheet as an allrounder – and probably as captain!

John Shepherd told me many times that I was his hero and role model when he was growing up and I am honoured that this was the case. I am certainly delighted to have known him as a friend for more than forty years – not least because I think that he shares my belief that sportsmen, no matter how successful or famous, need to live their lives with restraint and discipline as well as with flair and style. John never let his success go to his head – I am glad that his life in cricket has been recorded in this book and that his qualities as a human being shine through as well.

Everton Weekes
Barbados
February, 2009

Introduction

What do they know of cricket who only cricket know?
C.L.R.James, Beyond a Boundary

In his incomparable book on cricket, *Beyond a Boundary*, C.L.R.James poses a question that any writer or commentator on sport, indeed anyone who cares at all about matters sporting, should have at the front of their minds. Sport is not played in a parallel world apart from society but is an integral part of society – to look at sport without placing it in a wider social, political and economic context is to do an inadequate job. This applies especially to biography. Any 'Life in Cricket' is also a life in a societal context; and the sporting life often mirrors the world in which it is lived reflecting back in sharp relief its strengths and weaknesses, and absurdities and the injustices – as well as its joys and rewards.

The decision of the Association of Cricket Statisticians and Historians to move from its statistics-based 'Famous Cricketers' books to its new biographical 'Lives in Cricket' series (of which this book is part) is a welcome one. The statistics of a first-class cricketer's career are today easily retrievable online, especially at the incomparable CricketArchive website, but whilst there is a proliferation of books 'by' and about modern cricketing superstars (often absurdly premature 'cash-ins'), many fine players of the past are unlikely ever to attract the interest of commercial biography publishers. One such is John Shepherd. What attracted me to John was partly my long association as a supporter and member of Kent County Cricket Club (for whom he played a pivotal role in their success of the 1970s), but also that there is a real story to tell. The statistics of Shepherd's career are impressive and show how accurate, as well as prescient, The Cricket Society was in 1968 to give him their award as the leading allrounder in first-class cricket in England and also the aptness of *Wisden's* decision to choose him as one of their five 'Cricketers of the Year' in 1979. In the core twelve years of Shep's Kent career, from 1967 to 1978, he helped the county to no fewer than eleven trophies – an astonishing record. Shepherd's record is interesting enough as a spur to find out more about the man and his hinterland, but when you also consider his Barbadian roots and the fact that his sixteen years at Kent is the third-longest spell by an overseas Test player at an English county – beaten only by fellow Barbadians Gordon Greenidge's nineteen years and Roy Marshall's eighteen years at Hampshire – you see his unwavering loyalty. A 'Loyal Cavalier' indeed.

Loyalty is almost a forgotten attribute when we look at overseas players in modern county cricket. With a few exceptions, overseas Test players and

'Kolpak' players alike are mercenaries for hire to the highest bidder and John Shepherd's old county Kent has been in the forefront of this expedient approach. More than once an overseas player has been signed for just a few games or well short of a full season – compare that with Shepherd's sixteen years (or Asif Iqbal's fourteen years, for that matter) at Kent. In a thoughtful newspaper article, veteran sports writer Michael Henderson recently wrote about the truly great overseas players in county cricket and without exception these were the men who loyally served their counties for many seasons, not the short-term mercenaries. He included John Shepherd in his list and accurately wrote that Shep '... became part of the club fabric at Canterbury'.[1] The figures bear Henderson out. When, in 1992, *The Guardian* did an analysis of the contribution that overseas players had made to county cricket they showed that Shep's 976 wickets in the Championship put him at the top of the list of post-war overseas bowlers and third in the all-time rankings.[2] Derek Underwood states it plainly; he says that Shepherd was 'the mainstay of [the Kent] attack for years' and that essentially 'he was Kent'.[3] Times change, but the value of loyalty should be a constant – and it is also a two-way thing. Loyalty given and loyalty received are the two sides of the same coin and in this book we explore how this unfolded in John Shepherd's case. Virtually every player who was with Kent in John Shepherd's years spent a decade or more with the county. Some, like Shepherd himself, moved on to other counties – usually reluctantly, and some players, inevitably, did not quite make the grade – but in the main over these years it was a dressing room that morphed gently from one season to the next without major staffing disruptions. This had the massive benefit of creating a natural 'team first' emphasis – with nobody there just for a short-term fee for a few matches before moving on elsewhere – as all too often happens today. Shepherd also recognised the importance of the loyalty of spectators and supporters – in those halcyon days they were numbered in their tens of thousands, and that is just those that came to matches. Shep was always seen in the Supporters' Club tents during festival weeks and he regularly attended members' functions as well. In 1975 there were over eight thousand members of the county and the President at the time said that it may be necessary to 'consider putting a limit on the number of members'.[4] By 2007 membership had fallen to half of the 1975 figure.

John Shepherd's long career as a professional cricketer, from 1965 to 1989, spanned a time of almost unparalleled change in the game. The last Gentlemen *v* Players match took place only three years before Shepherd's Kent debut: and South Africa's banishment from the international cricketing arena spanned much of his career. The first one-day

1 Article in *The Guardian*, 2 September 2008.

2 Article in *The Guardian*, 6 June 1992. The two ahead of Shepherd on the all-time list are Jack Walsh of Leicestershire, and Ted McDonald of Lancashire. The next highest after Shep on the post-war list is Mike Procter of Gloucestershire, with 790 wickets.

3 Interview with the author, 4 September 2008.

4 Kent County Cricket Club Annual, 1975.

'international' match had not been played when John started his career - over 560 had taken place by the time he retired from the game. In his first Championship season with Kent Shepherd played in one match with the 46-year-old Godfrey Evans, who had started his career in 1939: in his last seasons, with Gloucestershire, Shepherd played with the young Jack Russell, who did not retire from the game until 2004 - a cricket line of nearly seventy years. Bob Willis described cricket in the 1970s as a time of 'Cricket Revolution' and Christopher Martin-Jenkins defined the period from 1963 to 1983 more prosaically as 'Cricket's Years of Change' - but, whether we see the arrival of Packer in 1977 and the explosion of one-day cricket which followed this as revolutionary or evolutionary, what is clear is that cricket would never be the same again. Sometimes John Shepherd was just a professional caught up in change: sometimes, as with Packer, he was a bystander (although he was close to the action as his Kent colleagues, Knott, Underwood and Woolmer were three of the six England players who committed early to Packer in 1977). And for a time, when he was one of only two non-white members of private cricket tours in South Africa between 1973 and 1976, he was uncomfortably in the spotlight.

While Shepherd's career years saw the game of cricket change beyond recognition, the same can be said for changes in the wider world that impinged upon his choice of career and his life. In the year of John's birth, 1943, the great West Indian Test cricketer Learie Constantine was overtly discriminated against at a London hotel and later successfully brought a civil action against the hotel for breach of contract and racial discrimination. But the 'Colour Bar' that he described in his 1954 book of that name did not suddenly go away in Britain and, as we shall see, it was also alive and 'well' in the Barbados in which John Shepherd was to grow up. Constantine said that 'Cricket in the West Indies is the most glaring example of the black man being kept in his place' and Jamaican Prime Minister and West Indies cricket historian, Michael Manley, wrote that Barbados had a 'class structure more rigid and more sternly reflective of colour barriers than any other Caribbean territory'.[5]

The racial and social divide in Barbados was particularly reflected in the club cricket world, where there was segregation on class and racial lines between the Barbados Cricket Association (BCA), which was under the management of the white 'planter-merchant' wealthy elite, and the Barbados Cricket League (BCL) which was predominantly black and poor. The BCA included clubs such as Wanderers and its bitter rival Pickwick which had been founded on racial grounds and remained selective on the grounds of colour until such discrimination was prohibited by law after 1957. This divide also extended to selection for the national team - Garry Sobers has written that ' ... in Barbados in the forties and early fifties, a coloured player had to be three times as good as a white player to play for the island'.[6] Very gradually, as independence approached and as the power

5 Michael Manley, *A History of West Indies Cricket*, Andre Deutsch, 1988.
6 Garry Sobers, *My Autobiography*, Headline, 2002.

began to shift, this did change,[7] but the hangover from the divided past was still a factor when John Shepherd started to play club cricket in the 1960s. The attitudes and behaviour of all members of touring sides to the West Indies had not always been beyond reproach either. On the 1953/54 MCC tour, for example, Len Hutton the England captain, was reported from the start of the tour as saying 'these black bastards don't like us'[8] - a casually offensive prejudice which hardly endeared the overwhelmingly black West Indian team to their visitors. In John Shepherd's youth, Barbados was a racially divided society and whilst he was never an activist he could see the signs all around him of 'them and us' - and they hurt. The white man had the house up on the hill with the pool and the servants and, as Shepherd left the country to pursue his professional career as a cricketer, he said to himself that one day he would return - and that he too would have a house on the hill.

But race wasn't the only discriminator that Shepherd was to encounter either at home or when he came to Kent. In the year of John's arrival at the county, 1965, the list of Kent's living Past Presidents included not just the fifth Lord Harris but the Lords Astor and Cornwallis, a Major-General and a couple of Colonels as well. In addition there was a powerful influence at the club of those who were members of the 'Band of Brothers', widely known as 'BB', an invitation-only and exclusive cricket club of great antiquity that played a full fixture list of matches against public schools like Tonbridge and King's Canterbury and elitist clubs such as the Eton Ramblers, the Hurlingham Club and I Zingari. Mike Denness[9] recalls that chairmen of Kent were nearly always 'BB' - as were leading figures such as the Cowdreys, Ames, David Clark, Stuart Chiesman, Jim Swanton and most committee members. Denness sees the BB involvement as counter-productive because it perpetuated the recently abolished amateur/professional distinctions amongst the players: the BB members would only talk to the 'amateurs' such as Cowdrey - it was very snobbish indeed. It also meant that hirings and firings were done neither by hired professional managers nor with any vestige of a consultative process - but by a cliquey and unelected elite. The separate changing rooms for the 'Gentlemen' and the 'Players' at some county grounds may have disappeared but there was at Kent, a clear distinction between the captain, M.C.Cowdrey, (of Tonbridge, Oxford University and Band of Brothers - who had always had his initials in front of his name and had regularly appeared for and captained the Gentlemen) and the 'players' making up the rest of the team. In the mid-sixties this was still a world of privilege and deference. Cowdrey was to be Shepherd's friend and mentor - the man who had the perception to see that Shepherd could be a success in county cricket despite his limited experience, and the man who made Shepherd feel at home as soon as he arrived in England. But there was always a patrician air

7 Grantley Adams became Barbados' first black Prime Minister in 1954.

8 Letter from E.W.Swanton to Viscount Cobham in May 1956, reported by David Rayvern Allen in *Jim: The Life of E.W.Swanton*, Aurum Press, 2004.

9 Interview with the author, 16 October 2008.

about the Kent captain and he was the archetypical establishment figure. Even as close a colleague as Derek Underwood (a man from a similar English middle-class background as Cowdrey) never called his captain 'Colin' over twenty years of playing together – and John Shepherd certainly never did. As Peter Oborne succinctly puts it: 'To get to grips with Cowdrey required an advanced understanding of the complexities of the English class system … .'[10] This led, as we shall see in Chapter Five, to moments when there was an ambiguity about Cowdrey and his own motivations which complicated matters for John Shepherd at a time of stress in the world of cricket.

John Shepherd was not just a consummate cricket professional but one of Kent's very few overseas players in the early post-war decades as well. For twenty seasons from 1946 to 1966 the Kent team was almost entirely made up of players who were qualified to play for England[11] and, Stuart Leary apart, Shepherd, in 1967, was the first major break with this tradition. Like his compatriots in other counties – Roy Marshall, Gordon Greenidge, Keith Boyce – Shepherd had to qualify for two years before he could play in Championship matches. This was a grounding which, whilst no doubt frustrating at times, was hugely beneficial as not only did Shepherd get used to English conditions away from the spotlight but it allowed him to settle in what must have been quite an alien environment.

From the start Shepherd was welcomed at Kent, not just at the County Cricket Club but also in the community at large. Shep reckons that he was one of only about five black people in Canterbury in 1965 but he cannot recall any moments of discrimination or difficulties caused by his race. This is not to say that there wasn't some unwitting and not always informed and casual prejudice around. Shepherd remembers a match against Northamptonshire when Kent's regular short-leg fieldsman was hit and Colin Cowdrey asked Shepherd to take his place saying: 'You guys [*i.e.* West Indians] have got better reflexes than we do.' Much more serious than this was an incident in 1971, when Kent were playing Glamorgan at Folkestone. The Kent side was taking the field when an elderly spectator, and one-time committee-member, patted him on the back and said, 'Good luck Sambo'. Unsurprisingly Shepherd performed poorly after this abuse[12] and also felt that the Kent captain in that match, the South African Stuart Leary, had been less than sympathetic to him after the incident. Shep eventually had to be calmed by Les Ames who said that he would insist on the member apologising – although this never happened. There are also some disturbing suggestions of prejudice on the part of some on the Kent committee when Shepherd, in many ways a strong candidate for the job, was overlooked for the Kent captaincy in 1978. Derek Underwood says that

---

10 Peter Oborne, *Basil D'Oliveira: Cricket and Conspiracy, the Untold Story*, Little, Brown, 2004.

11 The exceptions were South Africans Stuart Leary and Sid O'Linn, and Australians Anthony Jose and Jack Pettiford.

12 He bowled 22 overs for 77 runs as, ironically, the Guyanan Roy Fredericks scored a century and won the match for the visitors.

'... at that time I don't think that [Kent] would have wanted a West Indian captain'.[13] The light brown Asif Iqbal, who came from a privileged background on the Indian sub-continent[14] and was seen as something of a 'toff', was an entirely different matter. But it is important to nail the canard that prejudice was endemic in middle England – it certainly wasn't in Kent in the sixties and seventies anyway. Yorkshire in the 1980s was however a different matter and in 1984, in his last full year as a player, Shepherd and his Gloucestershire colleague David Lawrence were subjected to extreme racial abuse at a Sunday League match in Scarborough (see Chapter Eight) – this followed similar abuse directed at other West Indians at Yorkshire grounds over the years.[15]

The rewards given to cricketers in the early years of John Shepherd's career seem very measly when compared to the norms of today – even if we ignore the exceptional riches of the Indian Premier League and other million-dollar Twenty20 competitions. County professionals were paid only during the summer and pay for the younger player and uncapped was below the average wage of the times. For cricketers of Shepherd's ability, on the fringes of international recognition, the financial compensation was little better. In the West Indies, the Test match fees of, at best, $100 per game, were not much more than nominal and there was absolutely no security of employment. Couple this with the fact that there was no continuous international programme – the last Test match of the West Indians' England tour of 1969 finished on 15 July and their next Test did not start until 18 February 1971, a gap of 19 months – and there were no lucrative one-day matches in between either. So a professional cricketer had to ply his trade wherever he could, to make ends meet – unless he was of the old 'Gentlemen' class and had married well, like Cowdrey. It was the amateurishness of everything about domestic and international cricket that was to be challenged and eventually cracked in 1977 by Kerry Packer, but this earthquake in the game did not just ensure that cricketers would be properly paid in future. It also shattered once and for all the distinction in the English domestic game between the patrician, officer-class 'Gentlemen', like Cowdrey, and the rest who, though they played the game in part for the love of it, also had lives and families outside the game to sustain from their cricketing earnings. In the past the county professional was caught in a trap of having to accept remuneration which barely gave a living wage in the summer and less than that in the winter months – Derek Underwood remembers Kent being one of the 'stingiest' of all the counties.[16] The only carrot that was dangled in front of them was the 'benefit year' during which the most loyal county pros were able to build up a modest nest-egg which would help fund them when their playing days

13 Interview with the author, 24 September 2008.

14 Asif was born and educated in India but moved to Pakistan at the age of 18.

15 Report in *The Times*, 10 July 1984. The other West Indians were Gladstone Small, Norbert Philip and Vivian Richards.

16 Derek Underwood recalled, in an interview with the author, that all the players struggled to make ends meet: 'You would think twice about going out for a meal and try and save your meal allowance.'

were over. This system, described by Bob Willis[17] as 'semi-feudal', was at best paternalist and at worst patronising and divisive – and very reliant on the popularity and the efforts of the beneficiary. Post Packer, things even in slow-moving English domestic cricket began to change for the better – although the pace of change was a bit too fast for some. The editor of the Kent annual for 1978, the first year after Packer, records with some regret that 'Cricket ... is fast becoming a business which brings with it the inevitable controversies ... '.[18] No doubt the hundreds of previously under-rewarded professional cricketers around the world would have said, 'Not before time'.

The feudal nature of the county system applied also to the nature of the relationship between the club (represented by its volunteer and elitist committees) and the players who had little or no representation and virtually no security of employment. For example, the General Committee at Kent met in late 1966 to consider who amongst the players should be re-engaged for the 1967 season – the minuted entry in respect of Bob Wilson, who had been with the county since 1952, requires no further comment:

> R.C.Wilson. Not re-engaged. It was agreed, however, that should he report fit at the beginning of the 1967 season, the County might make use of his services on a match to match basis. It was further agreed that he be invited to practice on the St Lawrence Ground, during pre-season training.[19]

The Wilson instance is by no means an exceptional example of the crass handling of players by Kent's committees at the time. Derek Underwood puts it strongly: 'There was a total lack of sensitivity and of understanding what the life of a professional cricketer was all about by those running the club in the 1970s.'[20] Mike Denness says that things really began to change for the worse from 1974 onwards, when Les Ames, after a year as President in 1975, no longer held any formal position at the county. 'The committees were not interested in what the captain had to say,' says Denness[21] and – as we shall see – John Shepherd would be a victim of this incompetence and insensitivity. Most culpably there was a total failure of communication between the committees and the players – even with their captain.

Another contrast with modern times was the workload that professional cricketers had to undertake – and Shepherd, as an allrounder, worked as hard as anyone. In the statistical appendix to this book Shepherd's career year by year includes all the top-flight cricket that he played. Almost every

17 Bob Willis (with Patrick Murphy), *Cricket Revolution*, Sidgwick and Jackson, 1981.
18 Kent County Cricket Club Annual, 1978.
19 Minutes of Kent C.C.C. General Committee, 10 November 1966. Pre Packer this was the norm – as Mike Denness confirmed in an interview with the author, 16 October 2008.
20 Interview with the author, 24 September 2008.
21 Interview with the author, 16 October 2008.

Shep, after a full day's work.

year he would bowl around a thousand overs and play fifty or sixty innings – and there were others in the county game who worked as hard. 'Burn-out' was rare; indeed the term was unknown. There was also very little fitness training, apart from the occasional indoor circuit-training in the winter from which Kent's captain usually excused himself.[22] Shepherd was blessed with an almost ideal physique for a hard-working allrounder and he believes that he thrived on hard work rather than suffering from it: he was immensely strong in the upper body and, with powerful legs, could run in and bowl day after day without tiring. In 1983 Ivo Tennant wrote: 'A decade ago I was coached by Shepherd and well remember being awed by the size of his chest. His strength is huge. Woe betide the fieldsman who gets in his way when he winds himself up.'[23] Shepherd preferred the slightly greater effort of bowling 'up the slope' on those grounds where there was a difference, believing that it favoured his style to do so, for example from the Pavilion End at Canterbury. The back problem that cropped up during the Test matches in 1969 was to plague him on and off for the rest of his career but it never affected his commitment. Today, when the nominally far fitter cricket professionals seem very injury-prone, it might seem to some extraordinary that a professional cricketer could play at the top for twenty years without ever suffering a serious, career-interrupting injury. But as Shep explains you are often as fit as you feel; and if your commitment is unwavering and the side needs you then you play, even though it sometimes hurts. Derek Underwood says that Shepherd 'ran in every day for his county and bowled his heart out ... beyond the call of duty. He was a top pro ... he cared about his team ... he got us out of the mire time and time again. He'd even bowl fifty overs at Boycott – and that's enough to kill anybody off!'[24]

Nearly two decades after his first-class debut back in early 1965 John Shepherd was playing first-team cricket in the County Championship and the one-day competitions for the struggling county Gloucestershire. It is worth quoting *Wisden*'s description of Shepherd's 1984 season in full:

> In his 41st year John Shepherd was an example to all, with only John Lever among faster bowlers getting through more overs all summer. [He bowled 970 overs in all competitions]. Shepherd was still a match for the best, especially when conditions gave him some assistance. The help he gave to David Lawrence also began to show dividends.

The loyalty and effort that Shep, at the age of 40, was giving to his adopted county Gloucestershire was no less than he had given over sixteen years to Kent – a loyalty that, as we shall see, was not reciprocated when he was summarily deemed surplus to the hop county's requirements in 1981.

---

22 One memorable occasion excepted, when the television cameras had been invited in and Colin Cowdrey felt he should take part – which led to the captain being confined to his bed 'for a week' with pains all over his body!

23 Ivo Tennant, article in *The Times*, 16 June 1983.

24 Interview with the author, 16 October 2008.

Another key aspect of John Shepherd's value to the side was the rapport that he enjoyed with the crowd. Mike Denness recalls how he would usually have Shep fielding in front of the changing rooms at Canterbury and the crowd would expect to see him - and to have a light-hearted dialogue with him. This was illustrative of how the spectators would genuinely bond with the players - most of whom, at that time, were unwavering Kent loyalists through most of their playing days.[25] But the strongest feature of the Kent family was the genuine team bonding in the dressing room - and from the start John Shepherd was a fully accepted member of the team; his nationality and race was never an issue of any sort.

The journey that I have taken in researching and writing this tale of the cricket life of John Shepherd has been a richly rewarding one and I feel truly like a time traveller who has ventured back in time to a foreign country where they often do things very differently. The world of cricket has changed, but not beyond recognition - there are still twenty-two yards between the wickets and six balls in the over. The master-craftsmen with bat and ball still strut confidently on the stage as ever they did - and the cricket administrators still manage to mess things up as comprehensively as ever - albeit for slightly different reasons. Where snobbery, arrogance, prejudice and a love of the traditional orthodoxy were the sins of the committee-fodder in the days when John Shepherd was first a player, today it is the sin of greed, along with the offence of insensitivity, to which the cricket men in suits all too often succumb. Only an innocent would suggest that cricket should be played in a world where matters of money are secondary to the game itself - 'twas never thus. John Major, writing about cricket in England in the eighteenth century, said that 'money was to be the root of all progress'[26] - and that has certainly never changed in the centuries that have followed. But, as I have tried to show, another thing that has never changed is that though we may all agree that cricket is indeed 'more than a game' it is never right to compromise values just to allow that game to be played, however wonderful we may all agree that it is. To know the game of cricket well it is essential to know the wider world that not only surrounds it but impacts upon it. And in this respect perhaps we have not all advanced as much as we should and tried sufficiently hard to learn the lessons of history.

When Billy Griffith's Cricket Council said, in 1970, in respect of the planned South African tour to England that the tour would be 'not only a lawful event but ... [that] it is clearly the wish of the majority that the tour should take place,'[27] he was reflecting the widely-held view that if something is lawful and it is popular, then that is sufficient: for Griffith and the Council there was no uncomfortable moral dimension. Roll forward to the year 2003 over which period of thirty-three years you would

---

25 Interview with the author, 16 October 2008. Canterbury was, in its turn, one of Shepherd's more successful venues; he took 140 first-class wickets there at 23.94.

26 John Major, *More than a Game*, Harper Press, 2007.

27 Cricket Council statement of 19 April 1970, quoted in *Wisden*, 1971.

have thought that there was so much water having flowed under the bridge that by then cricket administrators would be different. Not always so! In South Africa, during the World Cup, England captain Nasser Hussain asked the then chief executive of the (now) *International* Cricket Council, Malcolm Speed, how his players could be asked to play in Zimbabwe ' ... when we don't think that it is morally right'. Hussain reported that when he said the word 'morally' Speed 'jumped at me. ... It was as if ... as soon as you used that word ... they would immediately tell us that we can't have morals in cricket.'[28] Plus ça change!

Similarly there has been little change in the tendency of some of those in charge of cricket to regard cricketers as disposable – just as Kent did back in 1981 with John Shepherd. Shepherd's crassly handled sacking by Kent, two years after his benefit and with sixteen years of loyal service behind him, was an inspiration for him to prove them wrong at his new county, Gloucestershire – which he certainly did. In 2008 Matt Walker, also like Shep a recent Kent beneficiary, was sacked peremptorily after eighteen seasons with the county. Walker said when he was quickly picked up by Essex: 'I've loved playing for Kent, but at this club people seem to think your time is running out when you get to a benefit year and that maybe you've already done your best work.'[29] Plus ça change again!

There is a lot of pompous rhetoric in cricket and there always has been. Cricket lovers often have a self-congratulatory air about them and they sometimes exude a sort of knowingness that whilst there are plenty of sports around none of them can compare with the 'noble game', which has a unique 'spirit' all of its own. I have always thought this to be poppycock, which is not to say that that there is not nobility in the sport, nor that it does not have players of principle playing it. One such was John Shepherd who always played the game unselfishly, putting team ahead of self, always walking if he nicked the ball and always treating colleagues and opponents alike with courtesy and consideration. The many distinguished ex-cricketers who have willingly talked to me about Shep have done so in part because they think that his life in cricket was noteworthy and that the story merits telling – I hope that I have done it justice. But as Derek Underwood put it, they also think that Shep is 'above all a great bloke'.'[30] The Australian Test cricketer Max Walker played with Shep in South Africa in 1976 and later wrote that Shepherd's

> ... company was an absolute joy. Blessed with a sharp wit and an engaging smile [he was] a man of immense character and courage, he steadfastly refused to believe that his colour should bar him from playing cricket anywhere. He would laugh at the idiosyncrasies of the whites and would laugh at being a black in a white society. He was a cricketer who liked to laugh a lot.[31]

---

28 Nasser Hussain, *Playing with Fire*, Michael Joseph, 2004.
29 Kent Online website, September 2008.
30 Derek Underwood, interview with the author, 16 October 2008.
31 Max Walker, *How to Hypnotise Chooks*, Gary Sparke, 1987.

And Tony Cozier, John Shepherd's distinguished Bajan compatriot, probably summed up everyone's opinions as well as anybody when he said to me that Shep was ' … an outstanding all-round cricketer and one of the game's true gentlemen.'[32]

Jim Swanton, writing about the three Barbadian 'Ws', Walcott, Worrell and Weekes, said that they had been 'Brought up in the cricket tradition of their island with a due sense of chivalry and good manners, they never slipped from grace, however tense the occasion, however strong the provocation' and then 'I can pay [John Shepherd] no higher compliment than to thank him for bringing to our Kentish fields a reflection of these qualities.'[33]

And it is to Barbados that we now journey to begin the story … .

---

32 Tony Cozier, e-mail to the author, 29 September 2008.
33 E.W.Swanton, Kings of Barbados, in *John Shepherd Benefit Souvenir*, 1979.

Chapter One
Belleplaine Boy

'... to come out of the wilderness into bright stars and don't get confused with the brightness, is a quality that does not exist with a lot of people'
Sir Everton Weekes on John Shepherd, January 2008

The pretty village of Belleplaine lies, as its name suggests, on a flat plain between two ranges of hills in the parish of St Andrew in the north-east of Barbados. St Andrew is famous for having the highest point on the island, Mount Hillaby at 1,116 feet, in its borders as well as the nearly 300-year-old Morgan Lewis sugar mill and the magnificent seventeenth-century St Andrew's Church. It is farming country, mostly sugar cane, and even today it has a tranquil air - a long way from the bustle of busy Bridgetown, the island's capital. As the crow flies Belleplaine is only 13 miles from the capital but today the journey takes over an hour along winding country roads and sixty years ago not every car on the island had quite the power to get over the hills at all. Belleplaine was once famous for being at the end of a railway line which ran from Bridgetown but the line closed in 1938. Today the village is off the tourist track except, perhaps, for the cricket pilgrim - for the Belleplaine area was the birthplace of three fine West Indian cricketers; Conrad Hunte, Keith Boyce and John Shepherd - and a few miles further north, in St Lucy, there was the home of that most lethal of fast bowlers Charlie Griffith. These were, in Griffith's phrase, the 'country boys from the north' who had a special camaraderie as they progressed though the Barbadian cricketing ranks - fearsome Charlie never once bowled a bouncer at his near neighbour Shepherd!

John Neil Shepherd was born on 9 November 1943 in a wooden house on the 'Rectory Corner' bend on the main road through the village, close to where the St Andrew's rectory once stood, and opposite a fine mahogany tree which stands today. The Shepherd birthplace, though, has gone. Through the branches of the tree there is a glimpse of a sports ground - the home of Belleplaine Sports Club and, from 1948, of Belleplaine Cricket Club. John's father, Ollie Vernon Shepherd, was a policeman and his mother, Kathleen Doughlin, was an accomplished seamstress, much in demand for her special skill as a maker of wedding dresses. In the 1940s life in Barbados for the majority of the population was not easy: infant mortality in the insanitary urban slums was the highest in the West Indies and the then colony had a feudal social structure little changed from Victorian times. In Belleplaine the land, as with all of rural Barbados, was owned by a small number of white or mixed-race (coloured) landlords and the majority of the black community, working the land as tenants on their behalf, was impoverished. Conrad Hunte describes how his grandmother would hoe the weeds around the young sugar cane roots and carry the cane on her head at harvest time to fill the donkey carts. As a public servant John Shepherd's father had a more secure and rather less arduous job than this - but there was little money to spare and life was often tough. It was a country life and a communal one, with neighbours sharing and bartering what they grew on their small patches of land - the Shepherds had such a patch on which sugar cane was grown and sold to provide a little extra income. The young John wanted for nothing - his mother was a good cook and the staple diet of breadfruit, rice, sweet potatoes and mangoes was healthy for a growing boy. John's parents split up when he was still young and he and his sister eventually became part of a larger family when his mother remarried and had three children with her second husband, Mortley Hutson. One of John Shepherd's half-brothers, Robert, was a good enough cricketer to play for Barbados youth - which suggests that the cricketing gene was maternal! As with most Barbadian families, religion played an important part in John's early life: every Sunday they went to St Andrew's Church together and as a child he attended Sunday school.

Although John's father was not a cricketer his grandfather[34] had been - a sufficiently good player to be selected for the 'Railway' team in the inter-war years - a rare achievement as Railway was mostly all white. Grandfather Shepherd was allegedly a magnificent hooker of the ball. John's father was a very good marksman and represented Barbados at this sport - and he always supported his son's soon-to-emerge ambitions as a cricketer. But the prime mover in the family was John's mother who encouraged her son from the start - which was when he went to the St Andrew's Church Boys' School just down the road from his home. The village junior school had a small and basic pitch and boundaries were twos and fours not fours and sixes, but the young players were enthusiastic and inventive. As a boy of six or seven John would cut the branches from the coconut palms to make a rudimentary bat - and a ball would be fabricated from a stone or cork centre, wrapped in cloth, bound in twine and dipped in bitumen to hold it together. The stumps were carved from the branches of trees or made from driftwood - or sometimes empty bottles would have to suffice. The cricket pitch was any piece of waste ground or on the beach - for the rugged north-east coast of the island, with its long stretch of fine but weather-beaten beaches, is only a short ride from Belleplaine and on Sundays everyone went to the shore and played beach cricket. On Bank Holidays there would be excursions to Foul Bay on the south-east coast of the island where games would be a little more organised on its beautiful, wide, white beach.

34 One of the most famous black professional cricketers in Barbados at the start of last century was William Shepherd, who played in fifteen first-class matches and umpired another eleven. Sadly no evidence exists that links John Shepherd to him!

The stimulus to embrace the game came also from young John's growing awareness of the feats of Barbadian cricketers in the West Indies team - especially in 1950 when the ever more exciting news from the West Indies tour of England crackled in on the wireless. There were six Barbadians in that tour party which was captained by one of them - John Goddard. But it was not the captain, a white Barbadian and scion of the Goddard's rum family, who thrilled the young Shepherd's senses. It was Frank Worrell, Clyde Walcott and Everton Weekes who were the batting backbone of the side and who scored four centuries between them. The West Indies won their first-ever series against England in England and the legend of calypso cricket was born - 'Cricket, Lovely Cricket'. The small but powerful Weekes particularly appealed to the young John - especially when news came in of his century and record stand with Frank Worrell in a winning cause at Trent Bridge. The three Ws and, for John, Weekes in particular, were real role models for this young country boy. True, Weekes was a city boy from Bridgetown, not a country boy like John - but his origins, born in a wooden chattel house in an urban slum, and his subsequent achievements were an inspiration - as they had also been for Conrad Hunte. In 1950 Shepherd remembers seeing a picture of the three Ws in a cricket magazine and he decided that Weekes was to be the man on whom he would model himself as he grew up - even to the extent, eventually, of copying his central-parting hairstyle and neat moustache.

Whilst the three Ws were at the top of the Barbados cricket pyramid, closer to home local boy Conrad Hunte was making everyone sit up and take note. In 1951 John Shepherd saw his close neighbour suddenly mature, scoring heavily for Belleplaine (including, in one match, hitting the longest six ever seen sailing into the distance over the pavilion), getting selected for the representative Barbados Cricket League match against their rivals in the Barbados Cricket Association (and scoring a century) and then, shortly afterwards, being chosen to play for the full Barbados side and scoring 63 in his debut first-class innings. If the nineteen-year-old Hunte from Shorey Village, just up the road, could make it, then why not another Belleplaine boy?

It was soon apparent that John Shepherd, young though he was, was indeed a gifted cricketer in the making. By the age of ten he was allowed occasionally to field in adult games on the Belleplaine ground and he began to learn his craft on that compact ground at his primary school. Cricket was beginning to be young John's passion and it was, as he now recalls, true that all 'he ever wanted to do was to play cricket'. But, under his mother's watchful eye, he did not neglect his schoolwork and in 1955 he passed the eleven plus and secured a scholarship to Alleyne School, one of Barbados' oldest secondary schools and conveniently located right in the centre of Belleplaine. Conrad Hunte had been a previous scholar at the school but, Hunte apart, the school had not much of a cricket tradition. It did, though, have a small pitch and cricket was firmly on the curriculum and the headmaster and sports masters were very keen - especially as old boy Hunte began to make his way in the game. A key influence was the cricket master John Gay who helped young John develop technically and, just as important, as an individual as he grew and moved from childhood into his teens. At about this time John and his family moved to a house just beyond the boundary of a new, larger Alleyne School cricket ground. In Barbados there is no 'off-season' - the wonderful climate allowed cricket to be played almost every day - so a busy ground it was as well. Very occasionally, a hurricane stopped play!

In May 1955, at the age of eleven, John saw his first Test match when the West Indies played Australia at the Kensington Oval. Sitting in the schoolboys' stand he saw the precocious young Garry Sobers, playing his third-ever Test and opening the batting, hit ten fours in an innings of 43, including four off consecutive balls from Ray Lindwall. 'That looks easy,' John thought to himself - and when he saw Lindwall clean bowl Sobers' opening partner J.K.C.Holt, with the stumps careering back to the wicket-keeper, he couldn't understand how the batsman, playing carefully forward, had missed the ball! That was John's first sight of the lethal effect of a fast and swinging ball.

In 1958 the tourists to the West Indies were Abdul Kardar's Pakistan and, at the First Test match at Bridgetown, John Shepherd saw his neighbour Conrad Hunte score a century in his first-ever Test innings and his hero Everton Weekes score 197. Then the visitors followed on with a deficit of 473 only to score 657 for eight declared in their second innings with Hanif Mohammed scoring 337 in over 16 hours at the crease. At that match John saw the lightning fast and ferocious Jamaican Roy Gilchrist running on to the field with his shirt sleeves rolled up to his shoulder and pumping the air in excitement at playing in his first home Test. Gilchrist opened the West Indies bowling to Hanif Mohammed who never saw the first few balls he received. At the same match the legendary slow left-armer Alf Valentine was sitting in the pavilion near to the schoolboy stand and was throwing a cricket ball from hand to hand, as spinners do. He saw John Shepherd watching him intently - Valentine threw him the ball. 'Here you are sonny', he said to John who despite his surprise had the presence of mind to catch it and mumble a 'thank you'. It was his first proper leather cricket ball - and the cricket bug was truly alive and well from that moment on in the young John Shepherd's soul.

At Alleyne School, John's cricket developed quickly and he was soon identified as the best cricketer at the school and was in the school team at 14 when his school report identified him presciently as a 'promising allrounder'. By the age of 17 he was made the captain of the cricket XI, as well as captain of the school. But although the school had a good academic record it was not one of the elite schools - those described by Keith Sandiford in his book of the same name as *The Cricket Nurseries of Colonial Barbados.*[35] These schools had more organised talent-spotting and links

35 Keith.A.P.Sandiford, *The Cricket Nurseries of Colonial Barbados*, University of the West Indies Press, 1999.

with the top clubs in the Barbados Cricket Association. However Conrad Hunte's burgeoning success perhaps drew more attention to Alleyne and in 1959 John Shepherd was spotted by the newly appointed Barbados government cricket coach - none other than John's boyhood hero Everton Weekes. Weekes, who was to oversee the development of young cricket talent on the island for eleven years, speaking in January 2008,[36] described the young Shepherd as 'part of that basket of youngsters that passed through my hands. I would say that he was, easily, one of not only the nicest, but one of the youngsters who listened very carefully to whatever I had to say.'

Part of Alleyne School, Belleplaine, in 2008.

The involvement of Weekes was crucial to John Shepherd's cricket progress. Not only did Weekes assist him technically but he also helped him focus on the aspects of the game at which he was most likely to excel. Weekes was a hands-on coach and dinned into Shepherd some of the key rudiments of good batting including calling, 'Yes', 'No', or 'Wait', and running between the wickets. As with many talented young cricketers John was experimenting with wicket-keeping, spin bowling and all the other cricketing arts - indeed for a time he was a wicket-keeper/batsman. It was as a keeper that John was called up for trials by the Barbados Cricket League for fixtures against the more elite Barbados Cricket Association. But in the school team that he captained Shepherd had two fast bowlers who he felt had rather suspect actions - so John decided to try and develop his medium-fast bowling so that he could open the bowling and keep the dodgy action bowlers just to one end!

36 Interview with the author in Barbados, 17 January 2008.

In 1961 Everton Weekes was asked to take a team of Barbados schoolboys to Jamaica and he selected John Shepherd to be part of the touring party - this was the first time, at the age of 17, that John had ever left the island. To mark his selection John's father gave him a top-of-the-range Stuart Surridge bat which, of course, was soon to sport a *genuine* Everton Weekes autograph. During the tour John's fast-medium bowling developed quickly. Everton Weekes remembers: 'He bowled more consistently and better than the rest - he bowled at the stumps and he was a great athlete ... he had his limitations, of course, but strengths as well ... to play within your own limitations is a strength.' Weekes was also impressed with the young Shepherd's attitude: 'John and I really talked quite a lot ... he listened'. John played at Sabina Park against a young Jamaican side which included Maurice Foster and a number of others who went on to play Test cricket.

When John Shepherd left Alleyne School he played club cricket for, and captained the Belleplaine village team in the Barbados Cricket League. In one match at Belleplaine versus Hillaby he scored a double century - 227, his highest-ever score - and as his talent blossomed further he decided, in 1964, to move to the long-established and prestigious Maple club in the Barbados Cricket Association competition. Everton Weekes had hoped that Shepherd might play for his club, Empire, but Maple on the west coast in the parish of St James was easier to travel to across the island from St Andrew. Now, for the first time, John was being tested against the highest class, playing against club teams with international players like Charlie Griffith, David Holford and Cammie Smith - and with success. This meant that he began to be noticed. Politicians and entertainers may come and go but there is no-one more famous in Barbados than a successful Bajan cricketer and soon John began to be known as a player of special allround promise. His photograph appeared in the papers and stories were written saying that he would soon play for the island team and was a potential future Barbados captain. But although he performed well at club level, including taking six wickets in an innings in an important match versus the Police at Kensington Oval, the breakthrough into the island team was much harder to achieve. Barbados had a phenomenally strong team at the time - the first six in the batting order were Hunte, Smith, Bynoe, Nurse, Sobers and Weekes, with Griffith and Hall opening the bowling - almost the complete side was comprised of Test cricketers. The Barbados Cricket League had occasional representative matches against the Barbados Cricket Association at the Kensington Oval, and John Shepherd played in a number of these matches and also captained the BCL team on one occasion. Whilst thoughts of a professional cricket career had been in John Shepherd's mind for a while, nevertheless on leaving school he expected to enter into teacher training and he had tentatively started down this career path. Then fate took a hand.

John Shepherd's cricket breakthrough was to come early in 1965 when, at the age of 21, he was selected to appear for Barbados, coached by Everton Weekes, against the International Cavaliers. The Cavaliers were a scratch side of mainly high-quality English players, augmented by a few from other

Belleplaine's cricket ground nowadays caters for footballers and basketball players as well as for cricketers.

countries, who were escaping the depths of the English winter for four weeks of sunshine cricket in the Caribbean. They were managed by Les Ames, the Kent secretary and manager, captained by Trevor Bailey, secretary and captain of Essex and there were eight other players with Test experience - including Colin Cowdrey, of Kent and England. The schedule included four first-class matches in Jamaica and Barbados against sides representing each of the islands. In the first match versus Barbados the Cavaliers faced a strong island team including the Test players Nurse, Sobers, White and Griffith. But in the second match, also a three-day game, these players were withdrawn in order that they could travel to Jamaica to prepare for the first West Indies *v* Australia Test match which was to start in a few days' time. Fellow Barbadians Conrad Hunte and Wesley Hall had also been called up for the Test side which was to have six Barbados players in it. This meant that there was an opportunity for those on the fringes of the Barbados team to be picked against the Cavaliers in the second match - among them the Belleplaine boys Keith Boyce and John Shepherd, who both made their first-class cricket debuts on 25 February 1965. In terms of personnel it was perhaps a Barbados 'B' side - but the record shows unequivocally that it was 'Barbados' - and that this was a proper first-class match!

Whilst a month in the sun and a little gentle honing of cricket skills was the main purpose of the Cavaliers' tour, a secondary objective, especially for Bailey, Ames and Cowdrey, was to keep an eye open for talented young cricketers who might be suitable for county cricket. Barbados was still a British colony at the time and its citizens had full British passports and right of residence in Britain - although prospective employers had to obtain a work permit and employment voucher for such 'Commonwealth immigrant' employees. Kent and Essex did not anticipate that this would be a problem - and nor was it. It was to be three years before the counties allowed themselves to offer an overseas player a playing contract without residential qualification, so in 1965 to bring a player to county cricket meant that they would have to qualify by residence - which took two years, during which time they could play Second Eleven, non-Championship and club cricket. Trevor Bailey, on behalf of Essex, and Ames and Cowdrey, on behalf of Kent, spoke with Everton Weekes about the availability of young players, and the two Weekes identified were Shepherd and Boyce. So the match was partly an audition, although neither player knew it at the time. The match itself was comparatively uneventful - more of an exhibition than a hard contest. In the Cavaliers' first innings Shepherd bowled 18 overs for 54 runs and took his first first-class wicket - that of Colin Ingleby-Mackenzie who was stand-in captain for the match. Shepherd batted at three in the Barbados first innings and scored 22 before being caught by Cowdrey off Jim Laker - not the first player ever to fall to that combination! In the Cavaliers' second innings John had similar figures to the first, one for 57 off 15 overs with the wicket of the great Hampshire Bajan Roy Marshall to his credit. And then in the final innings of the match, which was a draw, Shepherd scored 33 before being bowled by Trevor Bailey. A competent if not spectacular debut.

When the Cavaliers match had finished John Shepherd received a telephone call from Everton Weekes to tell him that Kent was interested in signing him and also that Essex were going to make Keith Boyce an offer. This came rather out of the blue to Shepherd. His mentor Weekes, and other heroes from Barbados, had all played professionally in England in the Lancashire leagues - and Shepherd had been thinking about this possibility himself if he decided to try and make a cricket career rather than become a school teacher which was his most likely alternative choice. Weekes was the intermediary and it was through him that Shepherd conveyed his interest back to Les Ames and Colin Cowdrey. With the benefit of hindsight it is intriguing to speculate on the extraordinarily foresighted judgment that the Kent and Essex representatives had in picking out these two players and bringing them to England - clearly the recommendation of Weekes was crucial. Sir Everton says today that when he saw Shepherd at the age of 18 he felt sure that he would play for the West Indies and no doubt when he spoke with Ames and Cowdrey back in 1965 he said something similar.

But before the final confirmation of an offer to John Shepherd could be made the General Committee of Kent County Cricket Club had to approve. The minutes[37] record, under the heading 'W. Indian Cricketer', that Les Ames

37 Minutes of Kent C.C.C. General Committee, 11 March 1965.

> ... reported that when he and the Captain, M.C.Cowdrey, were in Barbados, they were very impressed with an all rounder by the name of Shepherd. [Ames] wished to know whether the Committee, as a matter of principle, were in favour or not with the idea of importation. After a lively discussion, it was agreed that the Committee were in favour and if the Captain and the Secretary/Manager were in agreement, an approach could be made.

The financial risk attached to the 'importation' of Shepherd was removed when a generous Life Member of the county club, a Mr E.C.Wharton-Tigar, donated £500 to '... defray the expense of bringing J.Shepherd ... from Barbados'.[38] The offer that Kent now formally made to John Shepherd, whilst not munificent, was acceptable to him and so he started to prepare for the biggest adventure and challenge of his life. Part of that preparation was a long chat with Everton Weekes who told him the dos and the don'ts of playing cricket in England, learned from his long spell with Bacup in the Lancashire League and his three tours with the West Indies. Part of this advice was about dealing with the vagaries of (still) uncovered wickets. But more important was the advice to 'keep his nose clean' away from the cricket grounds! It was to be, as we have seen, John's first trip away from the island of Barbados – that one schoolboy tour to Jamaica excepted. But Everton Weekes was in no doubt that it was the right move for Shepherd at the time:

> He did the right thing at that time ... to go there and expand his knowledge, which he did I'm sure in so many different ways. ... He became a better bowler and a better batsman and ... he had to work harder there ... and conditions might not always be conducive to a man who's come from a warm country. It can be very cold in some places in England![39]

And cold it was. On leaving the aircraft at Heathrow, John Shepherd walked across the tarmac and saw his own breath for the first time in the near-freezing air. At the terminal it was Penny Cowdrey, Colin's wife, who was waiting to greet him. Mrs Cowdrey then took John to the family home, 'Kippin', in Hawthorne Road, Bickley – a detached house with large garden, complete with cricket net, in one of the most salubrious parts of north Kent. In the house there were some Golden Delicious apples in a bowl on a table. 'Do have an apple, John,' said Penny. 'Not likely,' thinks John under his breath, 'apples are red and I wouldn't eat a green mango so I'm not eating a green apple!' Colin Cowdrey himself emerged from the net in the garden along with the Kent coach Claude Lewis; they greeted John and soon afterwards he was taken to the local station to catch the train to Canterbury where he was met by Les Ames and taken to digs in Castle

---

38 Minutes of Kent C.C.C. General Committee, 25 June 1965. Wharton-Tigar was a distinguished ex-Special Services officer decorated for his actions in the Second World War, and later a successful businessman and a well-known cigarette card collector. He was President of Kent in 1977.

39 Interview with the author, February 2008.

Street where he was handed over to the tender care of a 'lovely old lady', Mrs Southern, who was to be his first landlady. Later that same long, long day Ames took John to the St Lawrence Ground, the home of Kent cricket, and showed him the indoor school where he was to report the following day. But John couldn't wait for that and, having been dropped at his digs by Ames, he retraced his steps back to the County Ground on his own and wandered into the indoor school again where he was invited to have a bowl by the club cricketers who were practising there. He knocked the stumps over with almost every ball and was then invited by his new friends after the session to have a drink with them in the Bat and Ball, the pub adjoining the ground. Later he at last returned to his digs and, in his freezing cold room, he put on both of the new cricket sweaters he had been given and got into his icy bed. He was so cold; a very long way from the warmth of his mother and his home: it was all so strange that on his first night in England he cried himself to sleep.

The Bajan influence.
Conrad Hunte, Garry Sobers and Everton Weekes were all key influences in Shepherd's early career in the Caribbean. All three were knighted.

Chapter Two
Kentish Apprentice

Shepherd ... from Barbados, is an all-rounder of considerable ability
Kent County Cricket Club Annual Report, 1965

1965

The Kent County Cricket Club that John Shepherd joined in April 1965 was long on ambition but short on achievement. The ambition came especially from the captain, Colin Cowdrey, who had taken over in 1957 but had so far failed to deliver the prize of a County Championship - or come near to doing so. The cupboard had been bare since 1913 and successive finishes of 14th, 8th, 13th, 10th, 11th, 11th, 13th and 7th under the Cowdrey leadership did not suggest that things were going to change dramatically. But behind the scenes there were promising developments - not least the emergence of a new generation of talented young players, some of whom were being fast-tracked into the first team. Future Test batsmen Brian Luckhurst and Mike Denness were beginning to find their feet after a faltering start, and they were joined by the precocious talents of Alan Knott and Derek Underwood - both still teenagers at the beginning of the 1965 season. The signing of Denness from Scotland in 1962 and of the tall fast bowler Norman Graham from Northumberland in 1964 showed that the county, under the Secretary/Manager Les Ames and Cowdrey, were casting their net widely and, of course, the arrival of John Shepherd was part of the process of being prepared not just to rely on Kentish men or men of Kent. The seventh position finish in 1964 was seen as a comparative success and there was optimism around the county. The arrival of the Gillette Cup competition in 1963 gave a second opportunity for a trophy for the first time and there was a growing recognition that the squad needed flexibility and allround talents down the order to succeed in both competitions.

John Shepherd was to have to wait two years before he could contribute to what was to be a resurgence of Kent cricket more spectacular than even the most optimistic supporter could have hoped for from the vantage point of the mid-1960s. But first he had to settle and adapt not just to the strangeness of green English wickets but to the unfamiliarity of his new home. A great help to him was the fact that Mike Denness and his wife Molly took him into their home - and he was to be a very welcome house-guest of theirs for the next eighteen months. But notwithstanding this kindness, he was for the first time in his life, at the age of 21, well out of his comfort zone, although he was soon relishing the challenges both cricketing and personal. His first match in Kent colours in the 1965 season was for the Second Eleven against Somerset at the Bowaters Sports Ground in Sittingbourne. It was a two-day match and Shepherd, in his first innings on English soil, scored 56 and took three wickets, in Somerset's first innings. The local press was enthusiastic about the debut: 'Shepherd ... created a very favourable impression whether batting, bowling or fielding, and his active approach to the game is a real object lesson.'[40] A few days later he played for the Club and Ground side at Maidstone against the Kent Police and, before the weather closed in, he scored 57 not out. Before May was out, there was another not-out half-century for the Club and Ground against London University.

Young hopeful.
John Shepherd in his first English season, 1965.

It was a promising start but one which owed little or nothing to coaching. The nets at the county ground were primarily for the benefit of the first-team players and, pre-season, the remainder of the squad, like Shepherd, was largely seen as bowling fodder for Cowdrey and the rest of the First Eleven batsmen. Under the Ames/Cowdrey regime Kent had dispensed with the services of their coach, Claude Lewis (who became the team's scorer) and, whilst the austere and authoritarian Second Eleven captain Colin Page also had a quasi-coaching role, there was no formal instruction at all. This meant that Shepherd really had to work out for himself how to cope with the strangeness of English conditions (the need to play forward on the softer greener wickets, in particular) and to demonstrate by his performances and his attitude that he should be in the team ahead of other candidates on the staff. Despite Kent having taken the initiative to bring Shepherd to England, his selection was by no means assured. After his initial half-centuries Shepherd, who had originally been seen by Kent as a batsman who could bowl, had a run of comparatively low scores as he tried to cope with the demands of English pitches in early summer.

As the 1965 season progressed into July and August, Shepherd began to deliver some consistent and important performances for the seconds. There were fifties against Surrey and Worcestershire and a fine allround match against Middlesex at Ealing when he took six wickets in the opposition's first innings and scored 51* in Kent's second innings. He also took charge in a valiant run-chase against Essex at Orsett – with 211 the

40 Report in *Kent Messenger*, 21 May 1965.

target they fell just short on 210 for nine, helped by a hard-hitting 79 from Shep which included 28 runs from one over bowled by Peter Lindsey. In August he was invited to take part in a forty-over testimonial match for Kent stalwart Dave Halfyard at Maidstone. Playing for the Cavaliers against Halfyard's XI, Shep helped his team to victory with the top score of 47 which won him a silver medallion and twenty guineas as Man of the Match. The match was televised by the BBC - Shepherd's first television appearance. Shepherd's bowling was progressing well and he followed Colin Page's mantra that he must always try to pitch the ball up and get the batsman to play at every ball; a simple message and one that was crucially important in Shepherd's allround development. Another part of Shepherd's progress as a bowler was his ability to mimic techniques that he saw others use successfully. For example he watched first-team bowlers Alan Brown and Alan Dixon in the nets and experimented with copying their styles and methods. John Shepherd was almost an ever-present in Kent's Second Eleven in his first season, scoring 735 runs at an average of 30.62 and taking 32 wickets at 26.59. He scored a further 256 runs at 42.66 and took 13 wickets at 10.38 for the Club and Ground. All in all, this was an excellent debut season at the club - not least if his unfamiliarity with English conditions is taken into account. He also fielded well, mainly at slip. He played whenever he could - including turning out regularly for the club side St Lawrence in Canterbury. The county, who had given Shepherd a guarantee of two years employment, must have been very pleased that what was clearly something of a gamble looked like it would pay off. Shepherd himself was not riddled with self-doubt - from the moment he arrived in England he expected to succeed in English cricket.

At the end of the 1965 season John Shepherd played in an International Cavaliers versus a West Indian XI match at Blackheath - the game was, as all of the Cavaliers matches were, mainly played for entertainment, but it was significant in that it was the first time he had appeared in West Indies colours. The West Indies side was captained by Sobers and included Kanhai and Gibbs - Shepherd acquitted himself well with an innings of 28.

Whilst adapting to the demands of professional cricket in England was one challenge that had to be met, assimilating to the very different surroundings of Kent and of England was no less important. In this respect it was friends at the county who played a crucial role. Twenty-year-old Alan Ealham was Shepherd's colleague in the Second Eleven and he became a close friend. Later Mike Denness, a more senior member of Kent's staff, and his wife Molly offered Shepherd a home at a time when he was occasionally feeling a bit lonely - the welcome he received into Denness's family life was warm and appreciated. Similarly the club captain Colin Cowdrey endeavoured to make Shepherd at home - including inviting him to spend Christmas Day with his family. Shepherd also made friends at St Lawrence Cricket Club (for whom he played a number of matches) - many from the rather well-heeled farming world in the Canterbury area. Clearly Shepherd's genial personality and openness made building friendships easy, but equally importantly he never then, nor hardly ever since, experienced any discrimination because of his colour. Kent County Cricket Club, and the world surrounding it, were truly welcoming places in those days.

Acclimatising in the English winter of 1965.

The Kent terms of employment covered the cricket season but, in the winter, players were expected to find employment and income to tide them through to the next season. And for John Shepherd this had to be local: he had to remain living in the county for two full years in order to qualify. He tried helping bring in the hops at harvest time - but lasted only one morning before the cold of an October day in the hop garden got the better of him. Through a St Lawrence CC friend he found a job at the Kent and Canterbury Hospital as an orderly on the orthopaedic ward which lasted him through that first English winter.

1966

The promise of the first season was built upon in 1966 when Shepherd was again a constant in the Second Eleven, scoring in eighteen matches, 873 runs at 31.17, and taking 53 wickets at 20.20, achievements reported by *Wisden* as 'grand all-round form'. He was described in the end of season report to Kent's Cricket sub-Committee as the 'outstanding player' - an accolade justified by his performances. About his fielding this report was especially glowing, saying that 'there can be few, if any, better allround fielders in first-class cricket today.' A feature of Shepherd's season was that he seems to have made a contribution in almost every match. If his batting failed he would chip in with wickets - and vice versa. His bowling was useful throughout the season, taking four or more wickets in an innings on seven occasions. One of these was Shepherd's first-class debut in England (and only his second-ever first-class match) when he played for the full county side against Oxford University in June. Batting at six he put on 38 runs with Colin Cowdrey before falling lbw to John Easter - he also opened the Kent bowling in that match, taking four wickets in the University's first innings and one in their second.

International Cavaliers taking the field at the start of their match with Kent at Canterbury on 29 May 1966. The players include, from left to right, Nawab of Pataudi, Godfrey Evans, Younis Ahmed, Keith Boyce and John Shepherd.

1967

The Kent playing squad was gradually evolving into a formidable and balanced outfit - stalwarts of the past like Peter Richardson and Dave Halfyard had gone and they would be joined by Bob Wilson and John Prodger over the next couple of years. Their replacements were mainly products of the Second Eleven, like Alan Ealham and Bob Woolmer, and - for the first time in 1967 - John Shepherd. The county, under Les Ames' shrewd management and Colin Cowdrey's captaincy, was steadily improving year on year with County Championship finishes of fifth in 1965 and fourth in 1966. Expectations for 1967 were high. After two successful seasons in the seconds, Shepherd's arrival in the first team was eagerly awaited - he had formally joined the playing staff at the end of his first year and now there was every expectation that he would cement a place in the first-choice eleven. Shepherd himself had no doubts and fully expected to make himself a fixture in the side - something which indeed he went on to achieve. However there was an initial disappointment when Kent went to Jersey in April for a pre-season short tour and Shepherd was not in the party - it was clear that his place in the First Eleven was perhaps not quite as assured as he assumed. In recognition of his arrival as a player now qualified to play in first-team competitions, Shepherd moved from a weekly wage of £15, paid only during the season, to an annual salary of £450.[41] (This compares with the salaries of the senior players like Denness and Underwood who were paid £700 p.a.)

John Shepherd's County Championship debut for Kent was at Trent Bridge on 29 April 1967 and in Nottinghamshire's first innings of 171 he took three for 53, with his first Championship wicket being that of his fellow West Indian Deryck Murray. On an awkward pitch Kent also struggled and when Shepherd came to the wicket they were in some trouble at 50 for five. Shepherd and Leary steadied the ship with a partnership of 87 for the sixth wicket and Shepherd went on to score 55, Kent's top score and an innings described in *Wisden* as 'defiant', out of a total of 169. The match petered out as a draw - with snow stopping play! Shepherd travelled to and from the match with Colin Cowdrey in the latter's elegant Jaguar - a gesture which was the Kent skipper's characteristically thoughtful welcome to the newcomer to the team. However the journey was not without its stresses as, on the way from the ground after the match, Cowdrey, in his enthusiasm to discuss the game, lost concentration, took a wrong turning and headed off in the wrong direction on the motorway. To Shepherd's alarm Cowdrey then crossed the central reservation - no barriers in those days - and completed an illegal U-turn to head back in the right direction!

In early May Kent played the Indian touring side at Canterbury and Shepherd scored what was then his highest first-class score of 70 not out against an attack that included the spin maestros Bishan Bedi and Bhaghwat Chandrasekhar - he also took the wickets of Farokh Engineer and Ajit Wadekar in the Indians' first innings. Next there was Shepherd's debut in competitive one-day cricket when he played his first Gillette Cup game against Essex. Whilst this debut was not particularly personally auspicious Kent won and then beat Surrey in the next round to qualify for a semi-final against Sussex at Canterbury in July. This was Shepherd's biggest match to date and nearly 17,000 spectators crammed into the St Lawrence Ground on a day blessed with fine weather. Kent batted first and John Snow removed Mike Denness quickly. Shepherd had been promoted to bat at number three and, with the ball flying around their heads, he and Brian Luckhurst then put on 135, with *Wisden* recording that ' ... the West Indian Shepherd punished the menacing Sussex attack right from the start of his innings' and John Woodcock in *The Times* saying, 'They have taken Shepherd to their hearts in Kent, and he responds to that with a flashing grin and as many boundaries as he can manage.'[42] Shepherd's 77 set up Kent who reached a match-winning total of 293 in their 60 overs with Cowdrey playing a 'majestic innings' of 78 'like a galleon in full sail,' according to Woodcock, albeit partly against the lesser bowlers, to win the Man of the Match award from Alec Bedser - an award that had seemed destined for Shepherd. At the end of the match Cowdrey had the grace to

41 Minutes of Kent C.C.C. Cricket sub-Committee, 10 November 1966.
42 John Woodcock, *The Times*, 20 July 1967.

apologise to Shepherd for pipping him to the honour. Derek Underwood remembers[43] how disappointed Shep had been as he had felt, with some justification, that he had done the hard work against the front-line bowlers but had had to concede the award to his captain who had played his fine innings when life was rather easier!

The Gillette final at Lord's in September was against Somerset and, batting in glorious sunshine, Kent seemed set for a formidable total when they were 129 for one at lunch, with Shepherd, again batting at three, going along nicely. But shortly after the interval there was a collapse with Shepherd falling for 30 and few of the rest of the team making much of a contribution. All out for 193. But it was, nevertheless, to be Kent's day once Shepherd, despite a pulled thigh muscle, had removed Somerset's top-scorer Robinson and the dangerous Australian Bill Alley. Shepherd had dropped his pace a yard or two because of a thigh strain and he bowled an accurate and very economical spell of two for 27 in twelve overs. Somerset were all out for 161 and so it was to be Kent's first trophy for 54 years – and new boy Shepherd had played a full part. A celebratory dinner for the team in the Carlton Club, with keen Kent supporter and Leader of the Opposition Edward Heath and other Tory grandees, was to follow. The apprenticeship was going well.

Whilst the Gillette Cup was the high spot of Kent and John Shepherd's year, the County Championship was only narrowly missed with Kent finishing second to Yorkshire. Shepherd was an ever-present in the side scoring 804 championship runs, at 23.64 and taking 48 wickets at 20.93. With the deadly Derek Underwood in the team Shepherd's chances to add to his wicket tally on poorer, uncovered wickets was limited – so it is all the more commendable that most of his wickets were taken on the better pitches. Among his personal moments to remember was an innings of 72, batting at three, against Hampshire at Maidstone which helped Kent to a comfortable innings victory: it was after this match that Shepherd was awarded his county cap in his full first season, then an unusual achievement. There was also a run of fine bowling performances in late August when he took 24 wickets in five games including a match-winning spell of four wickets in a couple of overs against Warwickshire which set up a Kent win. There was his then highest first-class score to celebrate in July when he scored 73 not out versus the Pakistani touring side and put on 142 in an unbroken partnership with Cowdrey. In the same match the Pakistani allrounder Asif Iqbal scored 41 in the tourists' first innings before he was out caught Knott bowled Shepherd. Asif was to return in another capacity for the 1968 season! In August Shepherd was joined in the Kent side by Godfrey Evans – twenty-three years his senior – as the great wicket-keeper helped out when the county was short. As Shepherd grew in confidence there was a contribution of some importance in almost every championship match with the bat or with the ball – or in some cases with both. The allrounder spot in the Kent side was seemingly assured although medium-pacer Alan

43 Interview with the author, 24 September 2008.

Colin Cowdrey presents John Shepherd with his Kent county cap at Mote Park, Maidstone, during the match with Hampshire in July 1967.

Kent taking the field against Sussex at Hastings in July 1967.
From left to right: John Shepherd, Mike Denness, Alan Brown, Stuart Leary, Norman Graham, Colin Cowdrey (captain), Derek Underwood, Brian Luckhurst, Alan Dixon, Bob Wilson and Alan Knott (wicketkeeper).
This was Shepherd's first full season in the Kent championship side.

Dixon with 569 runs and 89 wickets was something of a rival. In a light-hearted single-wicket tournament at Canterbury in early June it was Dixon who beat Shepherd in the semi-final before going on to win the competition. Shepherd's fielding was of a consistently good standard throughout the season and his tally of 33 Championship catches (mostly in the slips or leg slip) was second only to Cowdrey's.

By the end of the 1967 season John Shepherd had been in England for two and a half years and, with full qualification for Kent behind him, and a successful first season under his belt marked by the award of his county cap, it was time for a visit home to family, friends and to cricket in Barbados. He found a job as a clerk in Bridgetown civil court where he met a young woman, Terry Ford, four years his junior, who was working in the adjoining criminal court - also as a clerk. Terry was from St John, the parish next to St Andrew: they had a whirlwind romance and in March 1968, shortly before his return to England for the new county season and after nerve-racking interviews with Terry's distinguished father and intimidating mother, they became engaged.

John Shepherd and Terry Ford on their engagement in March 1968.

The cricket season 1967/68 in the West Indies was dominated by the visit of the English team, then still playing under the MCC banner and under Colin Cowdrey's captaincy. Expectations in the Caribbean were high as the West Indies could justifiably claim the title of unofficial world champions, having recently beaten England and India away and Australia at home. With the retirement of Conrad Hunte there was an opening up the order in the

West Indies side and there was speculation that John Shepherd's allround skills might just put him in the running for a Test place. Shepherd's mentor Everton Weekes met up with him and told him that there was a very good chance that he would be picked for the squad for the First Test in Trinidad in January. In the MCC tourists' very first game Shepherd was chosen to face them for Barbados Colts in a two-day match and a good performance would probably have led to his selection for the four-day President's Eleven match which followed it in Bridgetown – and then for the Test team. But fate was to take a hand. In MCC's first innings Shepherd bowled first change, taking a wicket and a catch – then, on New Year's Day he opened the innings for the Colts, putting on 74 with Geoff Greenidge before having to retire hurt after being hit in the face by a rising ball from David Brown. It was a serious injury, a depressed fracture, which threatened the sight in his left eye – he played no further part in the match and was detained in hospital for two weeks. This was one of the great 'might have beens' of John Shepherd's career. Had helmets been the norm the blow from Brown might have done no damage and it could have been Shepherd not Steve Camacho who got the selectors' nod later in the month in Port of Spain. As it was, Shepherd did not play again until he was selected for Barbados against MCC – a match which started on 22 February. In retrospect the return was too soon and both his bowling (none for 87 in 27 overs) and his batting (six and four) suggest he was not yet ready to recommence first-class cricket. Tony Cozier wrote later in the year that 'Shepherd's claims for a place [on the 1968/9 tour of Australia] were strong before he took a blow on the face from fast bowler David Brown. ... That accident set him back considerably and combined with an effort to make him into an opening batsman, saw him failing in the Barbados match. His claims virtually vanished and no one expected him to be named in April.'[44] Meanwhile England went on to win the Fourth Test and hang on for a draw in the Fifth to secure a famous series win – with Shepherd's friends and Kent team-mates Cowdrey and Knott playing the crucial part in both matches.

1968

When John Shepherd, newly engaged to be married and now very much in the thoughts of the West Indies selectors, returned to England at the beginning of the 1968 season, both his and Kent's expectations were high. In the back of Shepherd's mind was the possibility of being selected for the West Indies visit to England in 1969 and in the front of his mind was the determination to build on his personal success in his debut season and to help Kent to win their first County Championship after recent near-misses. Whilst the Championship win remained elusive, Shepherd was to have a personal *annus mirabilis* which showed that his extended Kent apprenticeship was finally over – by the end of the season his was always

44 Tony Cozier, article in the Barbados *Advocate-News*, 18 September 1968.

one of the first names on the teamsheet. And there was a new name alongside his - Kent, taking advantage of the new rule which allowed one overseas player per county who could play without needing to spend two years qualifying, had signed the Pakistani allrounder Asif Iqbal who had played an astonishing innings of 146 in the 1967 Oval Test match. (In the event, though, a back problem meant that Asif played primarily as a batsman in his first Kent year). The squad, under Cowdrey's rejuvenated leadership, with the Gillette Cup in their trophy cabinet and with class players in all departments, had high hopes.

The 1968 season was a watershed year for cricket on and especially off the field and Kent's captain was right in the thick of it throughout. At times in that fateful summer it was not England affairs that were a distraction to Cowdrey's ambitions for Kent, but the other way round. Regaining the Ashes and trying to preserve the planned winter tour to South Africa were Cowdrey's top priorities and Kent, for whom he played only 16 out of 30 matches, took second place. Whilst England completed a famous win over Australia at The Oval on 27 August (tying the series so the Ashes remained with Australia) Kent were ruing the fact that the absence of their captain along with Alan Knott and Derek Underwood (also in the Test side) had weakened the team at crucial moments throughout the summer - including their last match against Warwickshire which they had lost badly. On the same day as The Oval Test win a meeting of England selectors took place at Lord's to pick the touring side for South Africa - the meeting included both Cowdrey and the Kent manager Les Ames who had been appointed as manager for the planned South African tour. Whilst the details of that meeting remain sketchy it seems certain that Cowdrey and probably Ames were key players in ensuring that Basil D'Oliveira was not selected for the tour - a questionable cricketing decision but if your main objective was to keep the tour on track, as Cowdrey's was, understandable. The repercussion of D'Oliveira's non-selection, and the shambles that ensued when he was eventually chosen which led inexorably to the cancellation of the tour and then later to South Africa being excluded from Test cricket for 22 years, need not detain us here. However collateral damage was done, not just to the reputation of MCC and England cricket, to Cowdrey himself and to Kent's Championship ambitions, but also to John Shepherd - as we shall see. But at the beginning of the season these rather grubby events were months away and the optimism that always surrounds the start of a new cricket season was certainly rife in the garden of England when the sun shone at the start of the first match at Canterbury in early May.

The first Championship game of 1968 saw the Barbadian Shepherd and the man from Hyderabad, Asif, combine to skittle Lancashire for 69 in their first innings and Kent went on eventually to win the match by six wickets. Another unknown of the county's near-miss season is how many more games would have been won and bonus points garnered had Asif been fit enough more often to bowl in tandem with Shepherd. The pattern set in 1967 when Shepherd contributed with either bat or ball in almost every match continued in 1968. The month of June was particularly prolific, starting with Shepherd's maiden first-class century against Hampshire at Southampton. Coming to the wicket when Kent were in some trouble in their second innings, Shepherd scored 106* in two hours with 14 fours and 4 sixes to help see the county home for a draw. Reporting for *The Times*, the sharp-eyed John Woodcock spotted an on-field vignette which he related to his readers: '[The crowd] had the pleasure of watching some gay strokes by Shepherd, who made his maiden 100 after he had survived Kent's crisis, and if they were observant, they saw, at the fall of a wicket, [Barry] Richards of South Africa shaking Shepherd of Barbados by the hand.'[45] After taking five wickets for 22 in the next match against Cambridge University, Shepherd had another 'fifer' in the following match against Surrey at Blackheath and then four for 51 and five for 28 in the next two county matches. By the end of June Shepherd had already taken 42 first-class wickets and scored 422 first-class runs and commentators were beginning to talk about the possibility of a 'double' of 1,000 runs and 100 wickets in the season.

In mid-July Shepherd played against Yorkshire at Bradford, taking three for 31 in Yorkshire's first innings but he then suffered a rare injury – a pulled muscle that was to keep him out of the Kent side for three matches. (This gave the young Bob Woolmer his chance, which he took well, scoring 50* in his first innings for the county.) Looking back at the end of the season it was missing these three matches which cost Shepherd his chance of the double. But once he was back in the side he took nine wickets in a match versus Somerset and eight wickets in the next with Warwickshire, helping Kent to successive wins. After the Somerset match in late July Shep was third in the first-class bowling averages behind Illingworth and Underwood. In August there was a match at Dover against Nottinghamshire when Shepherd was trapped lbw for 19 by the great Garfield Sobers in the first innings – a favour that Shepherd returned by having his countryman caught for 17 in the visitors' first knock. In the Nottinghamshire second innings Sobers, angered by what he saw as negative batting by Kent, scored 105* in seventy-seven minutes, an innings which Shepherd now recalls as the most destructive he has ever seen. Nottinghamshire won the match comfortably with five overs to spare, thanks to Sobers' innings of genius.

In mid-August Kent played the touring Australians at Canterbury and, whilst the county side was comprehensively outplayed by a good allround Australian performance, Shepherd had a match to remember in more ways than one. He top-scored in Kent's first innings with 84, a knock in which he rode his luck somewhat with as many runs coming from good edges as from the middle. He was also the leading wicket-taker in the Aussie first innings with four for 47. But it was what happened after he was out to an Ian Chappell slip catch in the first innings that has stuck in John

45 John Woodcock in *The Times,* 4 June 1968. The mutual respect between Shepherd and Richards, which began during this match, was to be seen at a time of stress when Richards stood four-square behind Shepherd during the Currie Cup selection incident in Rhodesia in 1975. (See Chapter Five.)

SCORE CARD 6d.

Intervals:
Lunch 1.30 - 2.10
Tea usually 4.15

Umpires:
A. E. Alderman
O. W. Herman

Scorers:
C. Lewis
J. Mercer

HOST

FOLKESTONE WEEK — August 31st, September 1st and 2nd, 1968

KENT v. NORTHAMPTONSHIRE

Hours of Play:— 1st day 11.30-7.0 2nd day 2.0-7.0 3rd day 11.0-6.0 or 6.30

Kent won toss and elected to bat — **KENT WON**

KENT	1st Innings		2nd Innings	
1 **M H Denness**	c Milburn b Crump	20		
2 **G Johnson**	c Johnson b Durose	5	c and b Durose	0
‡3 **A Knott**	run out	73	b Crump	3
†4 **M C Cowdrey**	c Mushtaq b Crump	5	c Sully b Durose	66
5 **J N Shepherd**	c Johnson b Crump	170	c Durose b Crump	7
6 **S E Leary**	b Crump	3	c Johnson b Crump	49
7 **A Ealham**	c Prideaux b Durose	68		
8 **D L Underwood**	lbw b Durose	13		
9 **A L Dixon**	not out	82	not out	4
10 **A Brown**	c Scott b Sully	2		
11 **D M Sayer**	not out	6		
	B 1 LB 10	11	LB 2	2
	Total (for 9 wkts. dec.)	**458**	Total (for 5 wkts. dec.)	**131**

Runs at fall of wicket:—

1st Innings	1-12	2-43	3-75	4-163	5-181	6-345	7-351	8-415	9-437	10-
2nd Innings	1-2	2-13	3-105	4-118	5-131	6-	7-	8-	9-	10-

Bowling Analysis	O	M	R	W	Wd	Nb	O	M	R	W	Wd	Nb
Crump	32	4	114	4	....	....	15.3	4	42	3	....	....
Durose	21	3	79	3	....	....	13	3	63	2	....	....
Scott	10	1	66	0	....	....	....	....	....	....	....	....
Milburn	15	2	54	0	....	....	2	0	6	0	....	—
Sully	6.4	0	50	1	....	....	2	0	18	0	....	...
Mushtaq	16	1	84	0	....	....	....	....	....	....	....	....

NORTHANTS.	1st Innings		2nd Innings	
†1 **R M Prideaux**	c Knott b Brown	25	c Cowdrey b Underwood	67
2 **C Milburn**	c Leary b Brown	4	c Sayer b Brown	0
3 **A Lightfoot**	c Brown b Dixon	55	c and b Dixon	51
4 **Mushtaq Mohammad**	lbw b Johnson	87	c Cowdrey b Underwood	0
5 **B L Reynolds**	c Underwood b Shepherd	47	c Shepherd b Underwood	33
6 **H M Ackerman**	c Sub b Dixon	53	b Dixon	2
7 **B Crump**	c Knott b Shepherd	23	b Dixon	0
8 **M E Scott**	c Shepherd b Underwood	11	c Leary b Dixon	0
‡9 **L A Johnson**	b Underwood	4	c Leary b Underwood	0
10 **H Sully**	c and b Shepherd	1	c Shepherd b Underwood	5
11 **A J Durose**	not out	4	not out	21
	B 3 LB 3	6	B 4 LB 6	10
	Total	**325**	Total	**189**

Runs at fall of wicket:—

1st Innings	1-4	2-62	3-114	4-211	5-231	6-297	7-312	8-316	9-320	10-325
2nd Innings	1-0	2-122	3-122	4-124	5-124	6-127	7-161	8-161	9-161	10-189

Bowling Analysis	O	M	R	W	Wd	Nb	O	M	R	W	Wd	Nb
Brown	11	0	42	2	....	....	3	0	18	1	—	....
Sayer	17	2	55	0	....	....	5	1	31	0	—	....
Shepherd	23.5	4	92	3	....	—	7	1	21	0	....	....
Underwood	13	6	16	2	....	....	15.2	6	54	5	....	....
Dixon	16	7	30	2	—	....	15	3	55	4	....	....
Leary	10	0	43	0	—	....	....	....	....	....	....	....
Johnson	15	4	41	1	....	....	....	....	....	....	—	....

†Captain
‡Wicketkeeper

New ball due after 85 overs.

Championship Points Scoring System
For a win 10 points.
In a tie 5 points each side.
Drawn match where scores are equal 5 points to side batting fourth.
PLUS
First Innings Points as follows
1 point for each 25 runs above 150 in first 85 overs.
1 point for each 2 wickets taken in first 85 overs.

MEMBERSHIP
Join the K.C.C.C., details can be obtained from the office on the ground.

PORTABLE RADIOS
The Committee does not wish to prohibit the use of portable radio sets on Kent Grounds, but requests that they be not used during the hours of play.

The Kent County Cricket Annual is available on the ground price 2/6.

The History of Kent Cricket Appendix "H" (1946-1963) is available on the Ground. Price 5/-.

Completed Cards at end of each day's play.

Printed on the Ground by J. A. Jennings, Ltd., Canterbury.

Scorecard showing John Shepherd's highest first-class score, 170: Wisden thought his batting 'magnificent'. Despite this late-season win, Kent finished second in the Championship.

Shepherd's memory. As he passed the slip cordon on the way back to the pavilion Chappell, who has been memorably described as being 'no slouch in the profanity department',[46] sent him on his way with a vicious sledge which combined the 'f-word' with a racial slur. It was, as Shepherd now recalls, an extraordinary moment - the first time that anyone had sworn at him during a match and the first time he had been so abused. If Chappell's intention was to wind up the usually placid and imperturbable Shepherd he succeeded, because when Chappell came into bat, with Shepherd bowling, the latter tried to get his own back with aggressive short-pitched fast bowling which the Australian dealt with contemptuously as he scored an entertaining 57 - the visitors' top score. The ironic twist to this story is that some years later Shepherd and Chappell were to play together for the International Wanderers in South Africa and they became close friends - which they are still today.

Although John Shepherd may have been momentarily discomforted by Ian Chappell's abuse at Canterbury, it did not affect his performances for the rest of the season. The batting highlights were a century at Lord's versus Middlesex in a partnership of 189 with Cowdrey, who also scored a hundred. Shepherd reached his hundred by smashing fellow West Indian Harry Latchman into the grandstand for six, although Latchman got his revenge with the very next ball. In Shepherd's next innings, at Folkestone, he scored 170, including 5 sixes and 24 fours, in under three hours against Northamptonshire, taking Kent from 181 for 5 and setting up the foundations of an important win. There were to be, in total, ten centuries in Shepherd's first-class career and this innings was destined to be the highest of them. It was to be Shepherd's bowling talents which were to the fore in the next match when he took five for 30 to help bowl Glamorgan out for 103 and again set up another Kent win in their last championship match of the season. That match was John Shepherd's last first-class match of the season and he had now scored 1,157 runs at 29.66 and taken 96 wickets at 18.72 - tantalisingly close to the double. He could have joined his team-mates Knott and Underwood in the MCC side to play Yorkshire at Scarborough in an effort to get the final four wickets he needed - but after a long and at times tough season he decided to call it a day. No Kent player had completed a double since Les Todd in 1936 and had he not missed three matches in mid-season Shepherd would certainly have secured this rare achievement. Similarly, as in 1967, he often did not bowl many overs on the more helpful rain-affected wickets where the incomparable Derek Underwood held sway.[47]

In 1968 Kent won more Championship matches than any other county but they were well behind Yorkshire on bonus points and eventually finished runners-up for the second year running. John Shepherd's contribution with

46 William Buckland, *Pommies: English Cricket Through an Australian Lens*, Troubadour Publishing, 2008.

47 The 'double' has been achieved only twice since 1968, by Richard Hadlee in 1984 and by Franklyn Stephenson in 1988.

bat and ball and in the field - in addition he took 27 catches in first-class matches - was exceptional. *Wisden* described him as having a 'wonderful second summer' which ... 'more than fulfilled the high promise which he had shown in his first season.' This led to Shepherd being awarded by The Cricket Society the coveted Wetherall Award for the leading allrounder in the English first-class game - he was to be in illustrious company with Sobers, Hadlee, Illingworth, Imran Khan, Rice, Procter, and more recently Shane Warne - amongst others. Kent had found a star - and they had a bargain as well. Shepherd's basic salary in this outstanding year had been £700 p.a. (slightly more than the annual pay of an agricultural labourer and roughly equivalent to £17,100 in 2009 money) paid, of course, only during the cricketing months. But bargain or not, for Shepherd the apprenticeship was certainly over and Kent sealed their good fortune for the next three seasons by extending his contract until the end of 1971. So John Shepherd's career as a professional county cricketer had been well and truly launched, and in international cricket, testing times were ahead as well.

The Kentish influence.
Leslie Ames, Colin Cowdrey and Mike Denness all played a part in Shepherd's early career with Kent.

Chapter Three
Testing Times

I have always tried to play my cricket the Shep way. It saddens me ... that he has played no more than a handful of Test matches for his native West Indies. They are the losers.
Ian Botham, John Shepherd Benefit Souvenir, 1979

At the beginning of 1968 the West Indies could justifiably boast that they were unofficial cricket world champions. Successive series wins under Frank Worrell against India and England and then under Worrell's successor Garry Sobers against Australia, England again and India in India (that most difficult of Test match challenges) had placed them firmly at the top of the pile. But the home series loss to Colin Cowdrey's resolute England side in early 1968 dented the West Indies pride - not least that of Sobers who was criticised for the 'sporting' declaration in the Fourth Test which opened the opportunity for England to secure a famous victory. The West Indies should probably have at least tied that series, and might have won it narrowly, but nevertheless there were clear signs that the players who had lorded it over the rest of the world for so long were beginning to feel the strain and, in some cases, the pain of pushing ageing limbs and muscles to the limit. Sobers and Murray (Nottinghamshire), Kanhai and Gibbs (Warwickshire), and Lloyd (Lancashire) were all to play a full and tiring English county season in 1968 (37 matches in Sobers' case) before the next international challenge - a 23-match tour to Australia in 1968/69 including five Test matches. The fast-bowling partners Wes Hall and Charlie Griffith were looking as if they were reaching the end of their careers, as were the batsmen Nurse and Butcher. The team was in a state of flux and whilst places were not exactly up for grabs John Shepherd, after his good first season for Kent, had hopes that he would be in the West Indian party for the Australian tour when it was announced in April - fully five months before the team left for Australia. In the event the West Indies selectors ignored Shepherd's claims and picked a side primarily on the basis of past heroics rather than rawer promise. Had the team been selected nearer the departure date in October then surely Shepherd would have got the nod after his marvellous 1968 season for Kent? It may be that the selectors (especially Sobers himself) felt that with Sobers in the side there was no need for another allrounder and omitted Shepherd. The indications are that it was a close call and that Shepherd was unlucky to miss out. There was, as always, the wish to balance the side across the islands - a problem that has bedevilled West Indian selection frequently over the years. Writing in 1970,[48] Tony Cozier wrote of West Indies Test cricket: 'How can four separate independent nations and a number of semi-independent associated states play together as a team? The cynics may answer that they seldom do, but the fact remains that a group of 11 separate political entities combine ... to form the West Indies.' Nevertheless whilst other Test nations, in theory at least, made selections solely on merit in the West Indies a measure of inter-island balance was always consciously or unconsciously sought - and this may have affected Shepherd's chances for the Australian tour, and later.

As the West Indies were beginning the Test series in December 1968 John Shepherd was back home in Bridgetown preparing for his marriage to Terry Ford on the 14th of that month. He was also preparing to play, for the first time, for Barbados in the Shell Shield inter-island competition which was to take place in January and February 1969. This tournament was important to Shepherd both because of the honour attached to representing his country in a competitive domestic event for the first time and also because he felt that a good performance would put him firmly in the running for selection for the West Indian tour to England in the summer of 1969. He played in all four of Barbados' matches, scoring 186 runs, average 26.57, and taking seven wickets at 28.85 - modest performances with the main highlight being a knock of 73 against the eventual title winners Jamaica at the Kensington Oval.

Whilst the Shell Shield was under way, the West Indies tour of Australia was drawing to a close with the home side achieving a convincing 3-1 series win and, despite losing the First Test, eventually outclassing their opponents. It had not been a happy tour, with Sobers reported as being rather a detached leader, although batting at times quite brilliantly, and being out-thought by the dour but effective Australian captain Bill Lawry. Sobers' decision to ask Australia to bat first in the final Test backfired comprehensively as the Aussies piled up 619 in their first innings to set up a comfortable win. A drawn series with New Zealand was to follow and it was a tired and dispirited party, and an exhausted captain, that returned to the Caribbean at the end of March. The dilemma for the selectors was to decide how many of their number should be retained for the England tour which was due to start in a month's time. In the event they decided that it was time for a change and Nurse, Hall, Griffith, Holford, and Kanhai (who was injured) were not selected and a number of young players were able to get their first chance in the West Indies side - including John Shepherd.

Shepherd's selection was clearly based on the theory that his success so far in the English domestic game, and his familiarity with English conditions, would be an advantage to the West Indies squad - both on the pitch and in the dressing room. Garry Sobers rated Shepherd highly as a bowler on English wickets and had supported his selection. It may also be that Sobers had heard a rumour that Shepherd had been asked whether he might be

48 Article in *The Cricketer*, September 1970.

available, once qualified, for selection by England. The rumour was true - Shepherd had had quiet 'off the record' conversations with both Colin Cowdrey and Les Ames about this very possibility. He would not have been the first player born in the Caribbean to play for England (that was the famous Lord Harris), nor the first non-white England cricketer (that was K.S.Ranjitsinhji), but he would have been the first Afro-Caribbean England cricketer - an honour that was to go to his Bajan compatriot Roland Butcher in 1981. But Shepherd's selection for the 1969 England tour put paid to the possibility of qualifying for England and, in truth, he was very proud indeed to be putting on a West Indies blazer for the first time when he flew to England in March.

As well as the blazer John Shepherd had a leather cricket bag which carried the legend 'J.N.Shepherd West Indies' on its side. Travelling alone ahead of the tour party Shepherd reckons that this bag helped smooth his passage through the red channel at British Customs with bags full of wedding presents with him! His first non-cricketing task was to find a house to set up home with Terry who would be joining him later in the summer - a two-bedroomed semi-detached bungalow in Sturry, near Canterbury, was bought for the princely sum of £4,250 and this was to be the family home for twelve years.

The West Indies tour party, under Clyde Walcott's management and Garry Sobers' captaincy, arrived in England in April and John Shepherd proudly joined up with them at their London base at the Waldorf Hotel. Although it was his first tour, and he was a newcomer to the squad, Shepherd was not intimidated by the experience as he had an advantage over most of the others and that was his knowledge of English conditions - this gave him a particular credibility in the dressing room. And very English conditions indeed were the order of the day in one of the wetter Mays on record. On 10 May Colin Cowdrey was sitting in the dressing room at a rainy Canterbury and he wrote to John Shepherd to wish him well with the West Indies tour. The envelope was hand written by Cowdrey who addressed it to:

> John Shepherd, Esq.
> Champion of Kent on loan to the West Indies XI

- a characteristically genial gesture from the always thoughtful Kent skipper. Match after match was a rain-curtailed draw and John Shepherd had few chances to shine - with the notable exception of the match against Gloucestershire at Bristol when the county were skittled out in their first innings for 113, with Shepherd taking eight for 40 in what was destined to be his best-ever first-class bowling performance. He was selected for the match against MCC at Lord's in early June and was clearly in the selectors' minds for the First Test later that month.

The First Test took place at Old Trafford beginning on 12 June and, as he fervently hoped and expected, John Shepherd was in the team. At last the weather relented and having won the toss England rather ground their way to a large total - 413 off 197.5 overs, little more than two runs per over and

The West Indian line-up for their match with Lancashire at Old Trafford in early May, 1969.
Standing (l to r): Roy Fredericks, John Shepherd, Maurice Foster ,Charlie Davis, Pascall Roberts, Michael Findlay, Grayson Shillingford and Phil Blair.
Seated: Clive Lloyd, Jackie Hendriks (wk), Lance Gibbs (captain), Basil Butcher and Steve Camacho.
Of these players, only Gibbs and Shepherd had previously played a full season of first-class cricket in England.

taking ten hours to compile. In hot weather Shepherd and the others stuck at their task trying to break down obdurate batting from Boycott, Graveney, Edrich and D'Oliveira. Late in the innings the ball started to swing and Shepherd took five wickets in his first-ever bowl in a Test match (including his friend Alan Knott for a duck), and his name stands today proudly on the honours board in the old Pavilion to commemorate this feat. In fact until very recently[49] this performance by Shepherd stood as a record as the best by a West Indian bowler on debut. Shepherd had bowled 58.5 overs in oppressive heat in that first England innings and was taking a well-earned bath in the changing room late in the afternoon on the second day when there was a tap on his shoulder and he was told to pad up. The West Indies were 72 for four and it looked like he was going to be needed to bat (at No.8). Two more wickets fell and Shepherd, still a little damp from his bath and playing his first-ever Test innings, was 5 not out and the West Indies 104 for six when stumps were drawn. Overall the match was unfortunate for the West Indies who were dismissed for 147 and following

49 Darren Sammy, in his Test debut versus England at Old Trafford in 2007, took seven for 66 in the second innings.

England 411 for nine.
Shepherd has Barry Knight lbw for 31 at Old Trafford on 13 June 1969.
Sobers and Hendriks appeal.

on, for 275 to lose by ten wickets, Shepherd scored 9 and 13 batting at No.8.

The West Indies side in Shepherd's first Test match.
Standing (l to r): John Shepherd, Maurice Foster, Vanburn Holder, Clive Lloyd, Charlie Davis, Roy Fredericks.
Seated: Joey Carew, Jackie Hendriks (wk), Garry Sobers (captain), Lance Gibbs, Basil Butcher.

Later in June, at Lord's in the Second Test, the West Indies fared better, winning the toss and like England in the First Test grinding out a total - 380 in 158 overs. Shepherd batted for nearly two hours scoring 32 off 114 balls - including a six off a bouncer from David Brown, the bowler who had hit him such a blow on the face back in Barbados in December 1967. Jim Swanton recorded that Shepherd hooked Brown 'magnificently into the drinking populace on the site of the old Tavern'.[50] The sixth-wicket stand of 77 between Shepherd and Charlie Davis consolidated the West Indies' position and helped them to a decent total. When England batted, Shepherd played his part in reducing them to 61 for five by getting Boycott caught behind and taking a spectacular slip catch to dismiss D'Oliveira for nought off Sobers. England, however, recovered and reached 344 with Shepherd taking three for 74. The match was eventually drawn. During the England second innings Shepherd was fielding at slip when he felt a burning sensation in his back which was soon to need a visit to Harley Street and rest to get it right. But before that the West Indies were off to

50 E.W.Swanton, in *The Daily Telegraph*, 28 June 1969.

Northern Ireland where a match took place which has entered into the folklore of cricket, featuring in such books as David Mortimer's *Classic Cricket Clangers* and Andrew Ward's *Cricket's Strangest Matches*, among many others.

The regal touch. John Shepherd meeting the Queen during the Lord's Test in June 1969.

The cricket ground Holm Field is at Sion Mills, a small town on the A5 half way between Londonderry and Omagh in Northern Ireland. The journey to Sion Mills started after the Lord's Test when the West Indies rushed, after one of Nancy Doyle's[51] three-course meals, to catch their flight to Belfast and then a road journey to Londonderry. It was late and when they eventually arrived it was *very* late and further refreshments were not available. This refutes the myth that the reason that the Windies were not at their best the following day against Ireland was that they had dined and been entertained too liberally the night before! The next morning the West Indies struggled a bit before the game as their kit did not arrive with them but gradually things began to get in order and they batted first so that the Irish crowd could relish their batting skills. The wicket, however, was green - about as emerald green as a leprechaun's cloak - and the luck of the Irish was in play. Shepherd came to the wicket with the score at 8 runs for six wickets and departed for nought fairly soon after and, despite a robust last-wicket partnership of 13, the West Indies were all out for a less than challenging 25. It was the strangest cricket match in John Shepherd's long cricket career!

The Third Test match took place at Headingley in July and there were concerns in the West Indies camp about John Shepherd's fitness following the injury that he had sustained at Lord's. There was talk of calling up Shepherd's fellow Bajan and friend Keith Boyce, who was playing for Essex, to replace him. Sobers favoured this idea but his fellow selectors would not go with it and Shepherd kept his place. The West Indies put themselves in a strong position by bowling England out for 223 with Shepherd taking three for 43 in 24 overs despite bowling in considerable pain from his injury. But

51 Nancy Doyle was the châtelaine of the players' dining-room at Lord's for many years.

in their first own innings, with Shepherd absent hurt, they could only muster 161, and when England scored 240 in their second knock (with the West Indian attack hampered by Shepherd's absence) they were set an improbable 303 to win in the fourth innings of the match. But at 219 for three, with Butcher going strong (91 not out), they were in with more than a chance - but the cricket gods were not with them. Butcher was given out in controversial fashion; Sobers played an injudicious shot and was out for nought and Clive Lloyd followed immediately. Shepherd came in at No.8 with strapping all round his frame to try and reduce the back pain. He survived six balls before his great friends Knott and Underwood combined to send him back to the pavilion, caught behind. 'Contrived' might put it better for, to this day, Shepherd claims that he did not hit the ball - and even Derek Underwood will graciously admit, when pushed, that this was a lucky umpiring decision and that he really should be in the records with 296 not 297 Test wickets! Years later Basil D'Oliveira, who was fielding close to the wicket at the time of Shepherd's dismissal, confirmed privately to John that there had been no snick and that he had been very unlucky. The West Indies were bowled out for 272 to lose the match by 30 runs and the series 2-0.

It had not been an entirely happy tour for this transitional West Indies team. In the dressing room there were occasional squabbles and rivalries based on nationality and Shepherd remembers how the peacemaker was often the highly respected and senior member of the side, the Guyanan Lance Gibbs, rather than the captain. Sobers' leadership was always more by example on the field of play than hands-on guidance off it and in the Test series this example was modest - 150 runs at 30.00 and 11 wickets at 28.90. The tour established for Shepherd firm friendships that would endure - with his countryman Sobers and especially with the slightly younger Clive Lloyd. On reflection John Shepherd feels that he underachieved on the tour - especially his batting where he scored only 186 runs in 16 innings at an average of 13.28. He also feels that he should have taken more than 29 wickets in the 13 first-class matches in which he played, although his 12 wickets, at 22.16, in the Test matches was the best return by any bowler and he headed the averages comfortably. However as shrewd an observer as John Woodcock wrote in *The Cricketer* at the end of the series: 'Shepherd had come on splendidly as an allrounder'. Peter Short, who assisted Clyde Walcott on the tour and was in later life to be a president of the West Indies Cricket Board, said in the same magazine that 'John Shepherd's contribution must also be mentioned; West Indies have never had a bowler of Shepherd's type on tour in England. He proved invaluable under English conditions and was always considered a key member of the side.'

After the end of the tour, in mid-July, John Shepherd returned to Kent and he recalls vividly the contrast between the excitement and the packed arenas of the Test matches and the relative peace and quiet of the county game. It was something of a comedown and a return to reality - especially at grounds like Derby where the 'crowds' were usually pitifully small. The injury that he had picked up in the Second Test was taking a long time to heal and although he was available for Kent from late July he was only able to play in four championship matches and two in the one-day League. Mike Denness feels that the West Indies had 'bowled Shep into the ground'[52] during the Test series and certainly bowling 58.5 overs in England's first innings at Old Trafford followed by 43 overs in their first innings at Lord's was asking a lot – even for a man of Shepherd's legendary fitness and physical strength.

The West Indies had no fixtures between the end of the England tour in 1969 and the next scheduled home series beginning in February 1971. So at the end of the 1969 English season John Shepherd decided to stay in England and set up home in his new house in Sturry to try to establish the beginnings of a stable family life with Terry. He also needed to get fully fit for the 1970 season; a decision which paid off, as we shall see (Chapter Four) as he helped Kent to their first County Championship for 57 years, taking 84 wickets and scoring 695 runs in the process. Also during the 1970 season Shepherd was called up by the selectors[53] of the Rest of the World side which played five matches under Test match rules against England. He just missed out on selection for any of the matches and was particularly unlucky at Headingley where the green wicket seemed made for him. He was twelfth man for the last two matches at Headingley and The Oval.

After the successes of the 1970 season John decided to return to Barbados for the 1970/71 domestic season and, he hoped, to put himself again in contention for selection for the Test side. He had been told by Garry Sobers that he was to be part of the West Indies squad for the upcoming home Test series *v* India and that his fare back home was to be paid for by the West Indies board. Terry, who was pregnant, came with him. The first Shell Shield match was in January 1971 in St Lucia and whilst the match was under way, Terry phoned him from Barbados to say that there was a problem and that it looked as if the baby, only a week or so from its due date, had died in the womb. Hardly surprisingly Shepherd played little part in the match but he had to wait until the match was over before he could return to Barbados to be with his wife who had, in the meantime, lost the child. This was a tragedy that they and their families had to deal with and if John wanted to resume his cricket career he had to make himself available for selection immediately. The next match, against Guyana, was at the Kensington Oval only a week afterwards and Shepherd courageously played and acquitted himself well – as he did in the next match in Port of Spain and, back home, in Barbados's match against the Indian tourists when he took four wickets in the tourists' first innings. But Shepherd was not selected for the first three Test matches, and to comprehend this we need to understand West Indian cricket politics with a few selections taking place for each match which favoured candidates from the island

52 Interview with the author, 16 October 2008.
53 These were F.R.Brown (manager); G.S.Sobers (captain) and L.E.G.Ames.

where the Test was played. (The Jamaican Arthur Barrett played in the First Test at Kingston, for example). The Bajan Shepherd had to wait until the Fourth Test in Barbados for his 'turn'. The match was a high-scoring draw with Shepherd having little chance to shine with the bat but bowling economically (and taking a wicket) in each of the Indians' innings. He retained his place in the side for the Fifth Test where he again bowled well, taking three for 78 in 35 overs in India's first innings and two for 45 in their second. The young Sunil Gavaskar was Shepherd's last Test victim, clean bowled for 220, but his last Test innings was a mere nine runs when as an opening batsman he was out trying to get a run chase off the ground in the West Indies' second knock.

During the Test match in Trinidad John Shepherd's great friend and compatriot Keith Boyce said to him that he had been speaking to Dr Rudi Webster (also a Bajan) who was then helping the West Indies team. Webster told Boyce that he understood that Shepherd would never play for the West Indies again. Was he perceived as a rebel? Was there some hidden agenda? Was there a personality conflict or a mythical story doing the rounds that scuppered his chances? Was there some terrible mistake? To this day Shepherd does not know - but it was to be a prediction that sadly for him was to become true.

The West Indies' next series was at home against New Zealand in early 1972 and Shepherd was not asked to make himself available for that series by coming home for the 1972 Shell Shield competition, despite the fact that he had had another good season for Kent in 1971. Three West Indians active in county cricket (Lloyd, Fredericks and Holder) were brought back to the West Indies for the New Zealand visit all expenses paid, but all the others, including Shepherd, were advised that, whilst they would be considered if they returned home under their own steam, they would only have their travelling expenses paid if they were eventually selected for the Test team. West Indies cricket was seriously under-funded at the time - no doubt had more money been available, more England-based West Indians, like Shepherd, would have been brought home at the West Indies Board's expense. In the circumstances John Shepherd decided to stay in England for the 1971/72 winter.

For Shepherd a call from the West Indies selectors was also not to come for the visit of the Australians planned for February-April 1973 either. Along with fourteen other West Indians in county cricket he did receive a letter advising him of the terms that would apply should he decide to return to the Caribbean at his own expense in the hope of making the Test side. But, as in the previous winter, Shepherd decided to stay at home. Shepherd was also overlooked for the West Indies tour party to England in 1973 - and that was the final nail in the coffin of his international career.

Later in the 1970s, as the first cricket World Cup took place and one-day cricket expanded, Shepherd was again a logical choice, as one of the best allrounders in the world, for the West Indies team. But by then his involvement in Southern African cricket (Chapter Five) precluded this -

even if the unknown reason why he was excluded from 1971 onwards had faded as an issue.

In later years Garry Sobers said to John Shepherd that he, Shepherd, should have played far more matches for his country than he did. And Colin Cowdrey, who perhaps knew more about Shepherd's cricketing talents from close at hand than anybody, wrote that he was ' ... only sorry that he has not played more in Test cricket for he was clearly good enough to do so.'[54] Why did Shepherd not have the opportunity to achieve more than his five Test caps? Nobody seems really to know. Tony Cozier[55] thinks that Shepherd could have improved his chances by committing himself more to Barbados, something that the shrewd observer Barry Richards also feels: '... one wonders if he'd had the inclination to go back to the West Indies to play Shell Shield seriously, he might have played in more Tests than the handful in which he appeared.'[56] He was very unfortunate also with his timing. West Indies played their first limited-overs international in September 1973, shortly before Shepherd departed for the controversial D.H.Robins tour to South Africa. As Kent were to show over the years, to have an allrounder of Shepherd's talent in a one-day side was a real asset. He could well have been a key member of the West Indies one-day side over the remainder of the 1970s had things worked out differently, but that too was not to be.

*In full flow.
John Shepherd in characteristic style in 1969.*

54 Colin Cowdrey, *M.C.C: The Autobiography of a Cricketer*, Hodder and Stoughton, 1976.
55 Interview with the author, September 2008.
56 Barry Richards in *John Shepherd Benefit Souvenir*, 1979.

Chapter Four

We are the Champions

John Shepherd is a fine cricketer ... he is what English cricket now seems unable to produce, a genuine all rounder. He is a good, practical bat who is at his best when attacking, but perhaps an even better bowler – probably the best of his type that Kent have had since the war. On the quick side of medium, he swings the ball both ways, moves off the seam, varies his pace and has a particularly good fast ball. He is a brilliant field anywhere, but especially close in.

R.L.Arrowsmith in Kent: A History of County Cricket, 1971

1970

On 24 April 1970 Kent County Cricket Club held a dinner to celebrate its centenary at the Great Danes Hotel near Maidstone and John Shepherd, along with all the other players, was asked by the county captain Colin Cowdrey to take a bow and to be wished luck for the season ahead. After a promising run that included the Gillette Cup in 1967 and second-place finishes in the County Championship in 1967 and 1968, the county had slipped back in 1969, finishing tenth. Previewing the new season Les Ames referred to the return of Cowdrey, after injury, and Shepherd, and hoped that : ' ... these two fine cricketers [would] make the Centenary Year ... a memorable one by winning one of the competitions'.[57] Ames' words were echoed by the chief guest at the dinner, the Leader of the Opposition, Edward Heath, who reflected back on the 1906 season when Kent had won the championship and a General Election had brought in a Conservative Prime Minister – he hoped for the same in 1970.

County cricket was arranged in 1970 so that there were twenty-four three-day Championship matches and sixteen Sunday League games, plus the knock-out Gillette Cup and, in Kent's case, a couple of other first-class matches. The prize that all at the county wanted above any other was the Championship, which in 1969 had gone to Glamorgan for the second time in their history. As Les Ames said the Kent team had been unbalanced in 1969 and had underperformed – only Luckhurst averaged over 40 with the bat and the bowling suffered badly from the absence of Shepherd. Optimism for 1970 came not just from the return of Shepherd and Cowdrey but from the fact that the squad contained seven players of

---

57 Reported in *The Cricketer Spring Annual*, 1970.

indisputable international standard: Cowdrey, Denness, Luckhurst, Asif Iqbal, Knott, Underwood and Shepherd. Shepherd's role in the season was to be crucial. The English Test players were to be busy in the five 'Test' matches against a 'Rest of the World' team. The other experienced allrounder in the Kent squad, Alan Dixon, was absent through injury for the first two months. Support for John Shepherd was to come from the young Bob Woolmer who bowled well when given the chance, but much of the bowling burden was borne by Shepherd who was clearly now being seen by Kent as a 'bowling allrounder'.

The first Championship match in 1970 was against the new county champions at Swansea and Kent lost a low-scoring match by 46 runs - but Shepherd failed to emulate his namesake Don who took eight wickets. The first victory did not come until late May against Leicestershire, with Shepherd this time taking nine wickets (six for 89 in the second innings), but the county continued to struggle and went through June without a win. John Shepherd's season, however, was going well and by the end of June he had bowled 366 overs and taken 33 wickets. He had also made some major contributions with the bat, including a fine 105 against Hampshire at Portsmouth which rescued Kent from 177 for seven and took the county to a respectable first innings of 310 in an eventually drawn game. But Kent continued to stutter along, even falling to an Essex run-chase during Tunbridge Wells week after Cowdrey (106*) and Shepherd (60) scored quickly to set a seemingly challenging target (203 in two hours) which Essex comfortably reached. But at the end of June Kent were bottom of the County Championship table - some 70 points behind the then leaders Surrey.

The turnaround began in a match that started on 1 July when Kent, without their England Test stars, had an innings victory against Essex at Harlow - Shepherd again in fine form with five for 41 in the Essex first innings. This win was, however, to be followed by a disappointing loss against Middlesex at Lord's (Shepherd three for 54 and four for 67 notwithstanding) and a tame defeat at Canterbury to Sussex in the Gillette Cup was to follow. Kent's batting great, eighty-two-year-old Frank Woolley (who had been in the Kent side in 1913 when the Championship had last been won) was visiting the county from his home in Canada at the time of this debacle to see progress on the new stand at the St Lawrence Ground and was heard to say tetchily that the new stand was 'too good for this lot'. After this defeat Secretary/Manager Les Ames 'blew his top' in the dressing room and this helped transform an underperforming county into a winning team. Momentum began to gather with wins against Hampshire and Sussex and by the end of July Kent had 'climbed' to 13th in the table. John Shepherd was the mainstay of the bowling attack, illustrated by a drawn match at Sheffield when he took five for 123 in the only Yorkshire innings and bowled a phenomenal 52 overs with hardly a break. He also set up the win against Sussex at Hove, forcing the home side to follow on by taking five for 45 in 25 testing and economical overs. A further big wicket haul for Shepherd followed in a drawn match against Middlesex (six for 33) at

Lord's where he skilfully exploited helpful conditions - and then Kent really got into their stride with wins against Somerset, Gloucestershire (chasing down 340 to win), Surrey and Nottinghamshire by the end of August - with Shepherd playing his part throughout. By the end of August these wins had pulled Kent to second in the table, only twelve points behind Glamorgan and with two matches to play to Glamorgan's one.

Kent's final home Championship match was against Leicestershire at Folkestone starting on 2 September and their aim was not only to win but also to garner as many bonus points as they could in doing so. At 102 for two in their first innings Leicestershire were looking comfortable on a good wicket but then John Shepherd, having changed ends, took four wickets for nine runs in 21 balls and together with Bob Woolmer they dismissed their opponents for the addition of only 50 more runs and gained maximum bowling points (Shepherd five for 64). Kent batted aggressively right the way down the order and when Shepherd and Johnson combined to take 21 runs off the 85th over they secured an unprecedented eighth batting bonus point, with Shepherd hitting the last two balls for six (straight drives into the pavilion) and then a cover drive for four. Kent went on to force a convincing innings victory and their 23 points took them to the top of the table. In the final match, at The Oval, Kent needed only a handful of points to secure their first County Championship for 57 years and these duly came with Shepherd contributing three wickets as Kent gained four bowling points: four batting points were to follow in a rain-affected match.

The Kent side which won the County Championship in 1970, for the first time since 1913.
Standing (l to r): Len Kilby (masseur), Bob Woolmer, John Shepherd, Alan Brown, Norman Graham, John Dye, Graham Johnson, Asif Iqbal, Colin Page (coach) and Claude Lewis (scorer).
Front row: David Nicholls, Alan Knott (wk), Derek Underwood, Mike Denness, Colin Cowdrey (captain), Leslie Ames (secretary/manager), Stuart Leary, Brian Luckhurst and Alan Ealham.

For John Shepherd it had been a long, long season. He played in every Championship match, bowled a phenomenal 867.5 overs[58] and took 84 wickets at 26.70. In addition he played in 15 of the 16 Sunday League games, scoring 240 runs and taking 23 wickets in 114 overs, helping Kent to 12 wins and to the position of runners-up in the League. By the end of the Surrey Championship match this workload had taken its toll and the back problem that had plagued Shepherd since the 1969 Lord's Test match recurred – so it was a sore but happy man who joined in the celebrations in the dressing room with champagne supplied by Edward Heath, now Prime Minister, who joined in enthusiastically. Shepherd's contribution to Kent's championship success cannot be overestimated and *Wisden*'s eulogy that he 'performed magnificently' is justified. He was the leading wicket taker as well as a significant contributor with the bat – many of his 695 runs were scored down the order and when chasing crucial bonus points. Colin Cowdrey believed in being flexible with the batting order and Shepherd, in particular, was used as a sort of dispensable wild card, to be played as circumstances demanded. He also took 23 catches. The back muscle injury sustained in the Lord's Test of 1969 had forced Shepherd to modify his bowling action – but his performances belied any problems. The Championship win brought a further and rather more formal invitation from the Prime Minister – a gourmet celebratory dinner in 10 Downing Street. The boy from Belleplaine had come quite a long way.

1971

For Kent the triumph of 1970 had laid a firm foundation for what they hoped would be continued success in the years to come, a success that was based on certain crucial underpinning in terms of personnel. The side had world-class batting (Denness, Luckhurst, Asif, Cowdrey in his swansong years), attacking bowling (Underwood, Graham, Dye), and hardworking and solid allrounders (Woolmer, Shepherd, Johnson and Julien) – along with the best wicket-keeper in the world, Alan Knott. The personnel for 1971 was broadly the same as in the Championship-winning year, although with Alan Dixon's retirement Shepherd was now undisputedly the leading allrounder on the books. In Knott's view[59] Shepherd and the other allrounders were the main reason for Kent's pre-eminence in the 1970s – and there is no shrewder observer than a man who had to watch every ball bowled more closely than any other when Kent were in the field. 1971 was Cowdrey's twentieth season as a Kent player and it was to be his last as captain (he carried on as a player until 1975). Mike Denness was due to take over as captain in 1972 but a serious illness curtailed Cowdrey's season and Denness took charge halfway through the 1971 season.

---

58 In the 1970 first-class season only three bowlers, all of them spinners, bowled more first-class overs than John Shepherd's total of 890.5. His namesake, Don, of Glamorgan bowled 1,123.3; Fred Titmus of Middlesex, 1,106.3; and Norman Gifford of Worcestershire, 965.5.

59 Alan Knott, *It's Knott Cricket*, MacMillan, 1985.

In 1971 Shepherd began further to develop as a bowler. His natural ability was as a seamer - not a physical action but using his arm and shoulders to good effect; this was the style that got him his Test place and his good results in the Test matches were with balls that 'ducked into the batsman'. But at the beginning of the 1971 English season he chanced upon an MCC coaching manual and read in this book a description of how to bowl an **out**-swinger with the seam facing away to the slips - a ball which had hitherto not been in his armoury. He then worked on the delivery in the nets and in a one-to-one session with his friend Alan Knott. The out-swinging ball gradually became Shepherd's stock ball with his in-swinger becoming his main wicket-taking ball - because it surprised the batsman.[60] Clive Radley, who faced Shepherd many times for Middlesex, says that he never felt that he was ever 'in' against Shep's bowling because of his variation and this surprise element. In Radley's view, Shepherd was a wicket-taker rather than a defensive bowler and there were usually some hittable balls in his spell - but it was dangerous to be lulled into a false sense of security.[61] Shepherd dismissed Radley sixteen times in various Kent *v* Middlesex matches over the years. John Shepherd's swing variation worked particularly well with an older ball, say thirty overs old, and he believes that through most of his career he was a better bowler with the older ball than with the new ball. The slower ball was not one that he used often, but he did occasionally use the bouncer as a shock delivery. Essentially he was, in Derek Underwood's words, 'a persistent good line and length bowler ... with a speed [in mph] in the late seventies'[62] - although there were no cameras to check this in those days.

The first Championship match of the 1971 season was at Bradford where on a sticky wicket Underwood and Shepherd skittled Yorkshire twice to win by an innings, Shepherd taking seven wickets in his first first-class match of the year. As a tough and very full season progressed Shepherd chipped in with significant runs or wickets or both in almost all of the 47 matches that he played in the three main county competitions. He took four or more wickets in an innings on eight occasions and scored fifty or more seven times. But the real value came in the solidity and the reliability. Before the start of the 1972 season Shepherd was described in the Kent Annual as the 'war-horse' *[sic]* of the Kent attack and he gained the slightly patronising but no doubt well-meant plaudit that he 'remains optimistic and cheerful under all circumstances'.

The 'war-horse' bowled nearly 950 overs, took just under 100 wickets and scored 1,272 runs in first-class and limited-overs competitions in 1971 and was in many ways the fulcrum on which the Kent side was balanced, and in a dressing room where there were occasional tensions Shep was, at 26 years old, emerging as a steadying as well as cheerful influence. Highlights

---

60 In Shepherd's view the fashionable description today of a ball that 'reverse swings' is nothing more nor less than his 'in-swinger'. There is nothing new about the reverse swinging ball!

61 Interview with the author, 2 October 2008.

62 Interview with the author, 24 September 2008.

included a hard-hitting 76 against the Indian tourists whose attack had their spin-maestros Bedi, Venkat and Chandrasekar – he took six wickets in the same match. There was also a cultured 81, and a partnership of 105 in 100 minutes with Cowdrey on a green pitch at Southampton in June. In July Shepherd helped Kent to a good win against Lancashire at Southport, taking five for 60 in the second innings. With Cowdrey missing and Underwood and Knott on Test duty a weakened side struggled in the latter part of the season and in the end finished a respectable fourth in the County Championship. One remarkable near miss was in the match against Sussex at Eastbourne in August when a target of 219 in an hour plus twenty overs might have been reached had Mike Denness not broken his nose during the run chase. John Shepherd hit a rumbustious 32, including three sixes, to take Kent tantalisingly close. Later in the month Shepherd scored 72* in a partnership of 104 full of brilliant strokes with Asif Iqbal against Worcestershire at Folkestone. But fourth in the Championship was a disappointment after the heights of the previous year and Kent also slipped back in the Sunday League falling from runners-up to seventh. Shepherd made a major contribution in this competition with bat (415 runs at 34.58) and ball (26 wickets at an economical 17.07). A highlight was the match against Somerset at Canterbury in August, when Shepherd scored 46 to help build a respectable total and then took four for 20 to set up the win. Curiously Shepherd's bowling in first-class matches was less effective – 59 wickets at an average of 32.98 (compared with 86 at 26.98 the previous year). It may be that the workload (768 overs) took its toll. He was also hampered at times with an intercostal muscle strain, missing one or two matches as a result.

The highlight of Kent's 1971 season was a run in the Gillette Cup which took them to their second one-day final at Lord's, against Lancashire. The semi-final at Canterbury against Warwickshire was described as having drawn ' ... the largest and most enthusiastic crowd seen at Canterbury since Bradman's farewell match in 1948' and Shepherd's economical bowling (two for 29 in nine overs) was one of the key factors in a comfortable win for the home team. At Lord's in September, in front of 25,000 spectators, one of the great finals saw Shepherd again bowl economically – his 12 overs cost 38 runs and he also had the wicket of David Lloyd. Chasing a modest total of 225 to win Kent were in serious trouble when Shepherd joined Asif Iqbal at 105 for five. They steadied the ship but Shepherd was out for 18 having 'hung on courageously' despite being 'always ill at ease' and at 162 for six there seemed a platform for victory with Asif playing one of his great one-day innings. Asif took Kent tantalisingly close before falling to a wonder catch at mid-off by Lancashire skipper Jack Bond – after which Kent subsided and Lancashire deservedly won the trophy.[63]

Joining the Kent first-team squad in 1971, after a qualifying year in the Second XI, had been the 21-year-old Trinidadian allrounder Bernard Julien

---

63 Tony Pawson reporting on the Gillette Cup in *The Cricketer*, October 1971.

– a highly talented prospect who had been labelled the 'next Garry Sobers' – a tag that was, of course, to be impossible to live up to. Julien played in 26 Test matches for the West Indies as well as appearing on and off for seven years for Kent. Julien was initially put under the tender care of his fellow West Indian John Shepherd and he lived with the Shepherds for much of the season as he found his feet in Kent. Later Julien was to move permanently into 'The Monument', a Canterbury pub where away from the Shepherds' watchful eye he lived a rather more unrestrained life! Over the years Julien was burdened both with painful injuries and with difficulties in balancing his life as a professional sportsman with his natural joie de vivre. John Shepherd, whose room-mate he often was for away matches, helped him considerably through these difficulties. An even more eccentric room-mate was John's close friend Alan Knott who on one occasion woke a soundly sleeping Shepherd at five in the morning doing callisthenic exercises noisily on the spot – a similar problem had, in Knott's words, ' ... ended my rooming arrangements with Geoff Boycott' on England tours![64]

With his Test career behind him, to his great disappointment and mystification, John focused from 1972 onwards entirely on being a county professional, augmented, as we shall see, by occasional winter employment in Southern Africa and Australia. He was never to play for Barbados again either; his whole professional life was to revolve around Kent for the next eleven years. And that life was to be in a county programme in which one-day cricket was to play an ever more important part. At the end of the 1971 season Les Ames put the new commercial realities into sharp relief: 'In eight Sunday League games [this year] the paid attendances were 28,106, whilst 36 days in the County Championship brought in 31,414.'[65] Kent's modest profits of £7,345 in that year came substantially from an increase in membership, to around 7,000, in response to the 1970 Championship success. A new one-day competition, the Benson and Hedges Cup, was to be added to the Gillette Cup and the Sunday League from 1972 onwards and, as a world-class performer with bat and ball (and in the field), Shepherd was to

Signs of success.
Shepherd collects a new Cortina from a Ford dealer in 1971.

64 Alan Knott, *It's Knott Cricket*, MacMillan, 1985.
65 *The Cricketer Spring Annual*, 1972.

be almost an ever-present for Kent in all these various forms of the game for the next ten years.

1972

The 1972 season saw some important changes in Kent personnel with the retirement of Stuart Leary and the decision not to re-engage the pace bowlers John Dye and Alan Brown. With a full-time staff of 16, and with Test calls taking players away at key times, the burden on Shepherd and the rest of the county's professionals was considerable. In the event, letting 'Doc' Dye go was a big mistake[66] as the bowling lacked a cutting edge despite the heroics of Shepherd and the county's other main bowlers. There was also a permanent new captain as Mike Denness formally took up the reins after his half season in charge in 1971. Whilst Kent's bowling at times lacked penetration in the County Championship, the presence of Shepherd and the other fast-medium allrounders Woolmer and Julien proved to be ideal for the 40-over Sunday League. Shepherd's bowling workload was down a bit from the heroic 940 overs he had bowled in all matches in 1971: he still bowled almost 800 overs and took 87 wickets in 1972. Once again it was in the one-day competitions that he particularly flourished, conceding only 3.41 runs per over and taking 37 wickets in the shorter forms of the game. Kent's immense batting strength (Luckhurst, Knott, Asif, Cowdrey and Denness scored 5,000 runs between them at the top of the order and Ealham, Woolmer, Johnson and Nicholls a further 2,700 as middle-order batsmen) meant that in 1972 Shepherd was rarely called upon to make a significant contribution with the bat - he dropped down the order to No.8 in first-class matches.

In the County Championship a low-scoring game in June at Tunbridge Wells saw Shepherd take seven for 38 in Gloucestershire's first innings with a fine spell of swing bowling. In August he helped Kent to a narrow win at Worcester with three for 85 in the home side's first innings and remarkable figures of 24.5-15-24-5 in their second. In the one-day game the most extraordinary match was at Leyton in the Gillette Cup in early August. Kent had been dismissed for a paltry 137 and looked out of the match - especially when Essex reached 55 without loss in their innings. Then Shepherd came on to bowl - the fifth bowler that Mike Denness had turned to. Shepherd proceeded to take four wickets for no runs with 'beautifully controlled out-swingers' - and Essex eventually lost the match by ten runs. It was clearly a match-winning performance by Shep - but not to the adjudicator, Alan Ross, who inexplicably gave the award to Asif Iqbal who had top-scored with 52 and fielded well! Kent went on to reach the semi-finals of the Gillette Cup where they went down to Lancashire by seven runs and so just missed out on another Lord's final. The new Benson

66 John Dye moved to Northamptonshire where he took 75 wickets in the Championship at 18.13 - his best season ever. He was not to be the last professional to be surplus to Kent's requirements who went on to profit elsewhere, as we shall see!

and Hedges tournament was also a disappointment, with Kent failing to make the knock-out stages despite wins against Sussex and Essex. In the County Championship and Sunday League, however, a trophy beckoned as the season drew to its close. In the three-day tournament Kent finished runners-up to Warwickshire, but on the final day of the Sunday League a fine run of five wins had put Kent in with a chance, but needing to beat Worcestershire in the final match. This they duly achieved in front of a crowd of 12,000 at Canterbury. In those last six winning matches Shepherd took nine wickets in 48 overs and conceded only 160 runs in total (3.33 runs per over) - a significant contribution. He also played an important innings of 28* against rivals Leicestershire to help Kent to a total of 172 which was just enough for a crucial five-run win. That match also saw Shepherd get an unusual wicket - one of the very few stumpings in his long bowling career. Alan Knott, who was standing back, threw down the stumps to catch top-scorer Tolchard out of his ground.

1973

As a prelude to the 1973 season Kent, as Sunday League champions, were invited to tour the West Indies for a month in January to play forty-over matches against local sides. The county team was augmented by one or two players from other counties, including Mike Brearley and Keith Boyce, and they all had a jolly and perhaps not entirely serious few weeks away from the depths of an English winter. John Shepherd played in most of the matches, including those in Bridgetown where family and friends came to see him on what was once his home turf. Shepherd had a few good innings on the tour - including a 57* against Guyana and took his usual share of wickets. Kent had few victories on the tour but one was against Antigua where a young batsman of 'sound technique and bold method' impressed Colin Cowdrey who felt that he would 'play for the West Indies soon'. The batsman was Vivian Richards. Mike Brearley recalled the extensive hospitality of the tour and wondered at its end whether he was the first batsman to reach 1,000 *rums* before the end of January![67]

1972 had been Mike Denness' first full year as captain of Kent and the successes of that season hinted that he was moulding a very fine side indeed - building on the foundations laid by his predecessor. And so it was to prove as Denness proudly recorded in his autobiography: '... only in one of my five years as captain did Kent fail to win anything, and in two of those years we won two competitions.'[68] Expectations for the 1973 season were understandably high, with the one-day tournaments seen as being a potentially more fruitful hunting ground than the Championship. The playing staff contained no fewer than nine players who had already played international cricket (Denness, Cowdrey, Asif, Julien, Knott, Luckhurst, Underwood, Woolmer and Shepherd) and, although Test calls were to

67 *The Cricketer. Spring Annual*, 1973
68 Mike Denness, *I eclare,* Arthur Barker, 1977.

deprive the county of their services from time to time, there was sufficient strength in depth and cover available in the likes of Johnson, Nicholls, Graham and Ealham. As we have seen, John Shepherd had been overlooked by the West Indies in their selection of the party for a three-Test tour in the late summer (as he had been for the Australian visit to the Caribbean earlier in the year), although his compatriot and friend Keith Boyce and his county colleague Bernard Julien made the squad - and both were to perform outstandingly as the West Indies, under Rohan Kanhai, enjoyed their first series win for seven years. Knott, Underwood and Luckhurst served England in Test matches and Denness joined them as captain for the One Day Internationals, and Bernard Julien played for the West Indies in all their international matches on the tour. These absences meant that John Shepherd was the mainstay of the Kent side, playing in all 24 first-class matches, all but one of the seven B&H games, both Gillette Cup matches and 15 of the 16 Sunday League games.

In the County Championship, in which Kent were to finish a respectable fourth place, John Shepherd bowled 659.1 overs and took 78 wickets - more overs and more wickets than any other Kent bowler. Good performances in the four other Kent first-class matches took Shepherd's first-class wicket haul for the season to 92 from 800.3 overs, at 22.32. He also played 35 first-class innings scoring 803 runs at 25.93, including five fifties. Early season highlights included a five-wicket haul at Lord's against Middlesex in June when he bowled 19.5 overs on the trot and took five for 40 and an aggressive 57* with 2 sixes and 8 fours in a declaration, setting century partnership with Cowdrey against Hampshire at Tunbridge Wells later that month.

Shepherd's bowling flourished through most of the summer and from late June to the end of the season there was hardly a match in any of the competitions in which he did not take at least four wickets in an innings. In 25 matches under various rules in July, August and September he took a remarkable 85 wickets. In the Championship in early July he played in the emotional match at Maidstone against Surrey (taking four wickets in the Surrey first innings) in which Colin Cowdrey completed his one hundredth hundred in first-class cricket. Later in the month he had a fine spell of seam bowling against Middlesex who were fast becoming his favourite opponents. Shepherd's six for 127 in 33.3 overs included the wickets of Test players Radley, Brearley, Gomes and Murray. He also took five for 92 against Essex at Leyton, helping set up an improbable win after Kent had been dismissed for 81 in their first innings. This was to be followed by a match against Worcestershire in which Shepherd's allround talents were displayed at their best. He helped rescue Kent from a parlous 108 for six in their first innings by launching a ferocious assault on the Worcester bowling scoring 71 out of 94 in 65 minutes, including 6 sixes and 4 fours. Then when the opponents batted he opened the bowling and took four for 106 in 38 overs. A few days later Lancashire were the visitors to Folkestone and, batting at seven, Shep, in what *Wisden* called a 'brilliant display', scored 87 (4 sixes and 10 fours) in a successful chase for batting bonus points. Then to cap a stunning month Shepherd took five wickets in each innings against Leicestershire at Folkestone.

In one-day cricket in 1973 Kent not only retained their Sunday League crown but also won the Benson and Hedges Cup for the first time. The B&H campaign started with comfortable wins in three of the four Group games and then there was a quarter-final victory against Hampshire. The semi-final was against Essex at Canterbury where a crowd of 15,000 began to assemble at 5.30 in the morning! After Kent batted disappointingly Essex seemed on course for a win when the door to a Kent victory was opened by Shepherd as their opponents, chasing a modest 170 for a win, lost two wickets in an over including Turner to 'a marvellous diving catch by Knott'.[69] Essex subsided to 123 all out and Kent were on their way to a Lord's final for the third time, where they won a hard-fought match against Worcestershire by 39 runs.

The Sunday League was also a triumph for a Kent team who secured the retention of their title as early as 12 August, with two games still to play. John Shepherd played in all but one of the matches and bowled a full eight overs in most of them. His performances both with ball and bat were solid rather than spectacular - 151 runs at 30.20 and 10 wickets at 32.50. But whilst these aggregate results are unremarkable, they hide the occasional sparkling performance - none more so than in the match against Somerset at Canterbury when, coming in with Kent on 208 for four with two overs to go, he propelled the side to a total of 241 with a spectacular assault on his fellow Barbadian Hallam Moseley. Shep hit 26, including four sixes in one over, one of which was a straight drive which 'sent the ball soaring over the Frank Woolley stand - a feat only achieved twice before in the long cricketing memory of ... Les Ames.'[70] Over the season as a whole Shep, in all competitions for Kent, took 116 wickets and scored 1,040 runs - the modern double once again. He also won a trophy presented by *The People* newspaper to the cricketer who hit the most sixes in the season.

Kent's success in 1973 was very much a team effort and Mike Denness showed that his captaincy skills were especially suited to the one-day game. Denness' successful leadership of Kent led to his appointment as captain for the five-Test MCC tour of the West Indies in February to April 1974. Denness had his county friends and colleagues Knott and Underwood in the tour party with him and another Kent teammate in Bernard Julien in the opposing ranks. But John Shepherd's rather remote chance of being called up to face England by the West Indies selectors in recognition of his fine first-class season in 1973 were to be dealt a final and fatal blow. For in October, when the English season was over, Shepherd was to fly to South Africa as a member of the Derrick Robins tour party and to be granted the 'accolade' of 'honorary white man' for seven weeks.

69 John Woodcock in *The Times*, 28 June 1973
70 Dudley Moore in *Wisden*, 1974.

John Shepherd, well-trimmed as ever, receiving The People newspaper's six-hitting award from an unfeasibly hirsute Fred Trueman at the end of the 1973 season.

Chapter Five

Honorary White

Hindsight is a wonderful thing. With hindsight we can see that the isolation of apartheid South Africa in the 1980s and 1990s did the trick - it helped bring that wretched regime founded on ignorance, stupidity and selfishness to heel. With that hindsight we can also see that Wisden was on the wrong side for much of the period. It believed that visiting cricketers, repositories of enlightenment, (sic), could bring illumination to that benighted land. Phooey! Wisden's line - with that blessed hindsight - was misconceived. Apartheid in South Africa couldn't be tempered; it had to be dismantled.

Stephen Moss (editor), Wisden Anthology: 1978–2006

As we have seen in Chapter Two, the 'D'Oliveira affair' of 1968 had divided the world of cricket. John Shepherd's Kent captain, Colin Cowdrey, and the putative manager of the cancelled 1968/69 South African tour, Kent's Les Ames, had tried to keep that tour on track and they had also been supporters of the 1970 South African visit to England. Cowdrey was one of the many well-known figures who supported an appeal to set up a fund, 'The 1970 Cricket Fund', intended to pay for police protection at 1970 tour matches. The fund had wide support including, significantly as it turned out later, that of the chairman of Coventry City FC, Derrick Robins. It is true to say that the overwhelming majority of cricketers, cricket administrators and cricket followers were opposed to the isolation of South Africa in sport.[71] For example a Special General Meeting of Kent County Cricket Club was held at the request of a member who moved that no players in the Kent squad take part in any fixtures against the 1970 South African tourists, but this was defeated by a 'large majority'. Whilst the cricket 'establishment' wanted to keep South Africa in the fold, even at a time when there had been little or no progress towards multi-racial cricket in that then benighted country, the wider opposition to the tour in Britain was strong - opposition which included some cricket notables like the broadcaster John Arlott, former Test cricketer the Reverend David Sheppard and the 26-year-old Mike Brearley. Amongst the tour's most vocal opponents in the world of cricket outside England had, unsurprisingly, been the West Indians whose Cricket Board had formally said that if the tour went ahead it would do

71 Supporters of the fund included Brian Close, Jack Bannister, Alec Bedser, the Duke of Norfolk, Rachel Heyhoe, and Tony Lewis; see Jack Williams, *Cricket and Race*, Berg, 2001.

'irreparable harm'. On 22 May 1970, the tour was cancelled following British Government 'instructions'.[72]

In the early summer of 1970 the West Indies Cricket Board of Control sought further to clarify its own position regarding the involvement of West Indian players in South Africa. They issued a statement which whilst deploring apartheid also made it clear that in the Board's view it was a matter for individual conscience. They said that the Board:

> would not attempt to dictate to any player on the question of whether he should play against South Africa, nevertheless the Board would deplore any attempt to bring pressure to bear on any West Indian player to participate in any match involving South Africa against his conscience.[73]

This statement was soon to be tested – albeit in South Africa's ideologically similar neighbour, the rebel British colony of Rhodesia. The West Indian captain Garry Sobers accepted an invitation to partner the South African Ali Bacher in a double-wicket tournament in Rhodesia, having failed to consult with anyone in the West Indies Board on the matter – and he duly spent a couple of days in that country in September. Sobers' participation caused a furore across the West Indies, not least because he met with Ian Smith, the Prime Minister of what was a rebel state and against which United Nations sanctions applied. Sobers freely admitted that he did it for the money (£600) and he was certainly naïve about the political ramifications of his decision. In the end, and after apologies and a bit of eating of humble pie, the tumult blew over – for him at least.

Following the cancellation of the 1970 South African tour to England, the Australian cricket authorities had to consider their position in respect of a planned Aussie tour to the Republic in 1971/72. They eventually decided not to proceed with that tour – albeit mainly on the grounds of security and safety rather from a morally principled standpoint. Not deterred by this, Colin Cowdrey was personally determined to keep the door to South Africa as open as possible, and proposed a private tour of an 'England Invitation team' to take place in March and April 1972 and rather audaciously planned to include not just Basil D'Oliveira but also the non-whites John Shepherd, Asif Iqbal, Harry Latchman, Majid Khan, Ron Headley and Bernard Julian in the multi-racial tour party![74] The non-white cricket bodies in South Africa were adamantly opposed to Cowdrey's initiative and put

72 These 'instructions' were cast in singularly diplomatic language. The key sentence in the letter from the Home Secretary, James Callaghan, to the Chairman of the Cricket Council read: 'The Government have come to the conclusion … that on the grounds of broad public policy they must request the Cricket Council to withdraw their invitation to the South African Cricket Association, and I should be grateful if you would put this request before the Council.'

73 Statement by the West Indies Cricket Board, reported by Tony Cozier in *The Cricketer* September 1970.

74 Reported in *The Guardian*, 10 January 1972.

pressure on D'Oliveira to withdraw - which he duly did and the tour plans collapsed as a result.

The fundamental question that was to be in play over the long years of South Africa's cricket isolation was, nominally in any case, not that of the rights or wrongs of apartheid. With few exceptions those who sought to keep the door open ritually expressed their opposition to the apartheid system but they did not see that this opposition should be expressed in a boycott. Cowdrey, for example, said in his 1976 autobiography: '[The South Africans] have had enough of the admonishing finger; much more will be achieved by warmth and goodwill from outside'.[75] Four years later Ray Illingworth was to say that one of his 'earnest wishes' was 'to see South Africa back in Test cricket'. Illingworth went on to say that 'The South African authorities were asked to achieve greater integration of black and Cape Coloured players and they did it.'[76] And in his 1984 autobiography[77] Bob Woolmer, in a chapter called 'No to Apartheid, Yes to Cricket' said '... apartheid is heinous, but South Africa should be brought back into Test cricket and should have been permitted to return years ago'. He went on to say that 'Slogans such as "You can't play normal sport in an abnormal society" ... are merely glib.' The contrary position was perhaps best expressed by John Arlott who in a debate in November 1969 said:

> It is political commitment and political belief that can make a man think that his opponent's views are so obnoxious that he will abstain from playing any game against him, as a protest against what the other man believes and also, lest it be assumed that by taking part in any activity with the supporters of that view, he gives his tacit approval.[78]

At the same debate Wilf Wooller put the case that some in the world of cricket felt strongly - which was that sport, and cricket especially, was being discriminated against. Wooller said: 'Why should MPs suggest we should not play against South Africa when they're [big business] busy trading with South Africa?' He added: 'If you bring politics into our sport, you're going to destroy the last bastion of sanity we have.'

On the one hand many in the cricket world just wanted to play cricket and wanted the game of cricket somehow to be divorced from politics. Over time apologists for continuing cricketing ties latched on to the fact that some progress was being made towards the breaking down of the racial barriers in cricket and argued that more contact, especially actually playing against the South Africans, would further this process. On the other hand those who strongly opposed such contact did so on the not unreasonable grounds that to play cricket in or with a country that practised the

---

75 Colin Cowdrey, *M.C.C.: The Autobiography of a Cricketer*, Hodder and Stoughton, 1976.

76 Ray Illingworth, *Yorkshire and Back*, Queen Anne Press, 1980.

77 Bob Woolmer, *Pirate and Rebel?*, Arthur Barker, 1984. Bob was not a politician. He said in the same book that 'If the country were to be ruled overnight by the African community without the skills of the white man, it would be difficult to see how it could survive...'

78 Quoted by David Rayvern Allen, in *Arlott*, HarperCollins, 1994.

abomination of apartheid would be an affront, notwithstanding the fact that the cricketing authorities had created small islands of multiracial integration in a country that was otherwise overwhelmingly, and constitutionally, divided on racial grounds. As Peter Hain put it, 'Sport can no more be considered in isolation from the society in which it occurs, than can other human activities.'[79]

By 1973 those who supported continuing sporting ties had to bow to the inevitable, at least as far as official tours to the Republic of South Africa were concerned. But the maverick businessman and sports enthusiast Derrick Harold Robins thought otherwise and he had the money to put his thoughts into practice. Robins was a wicket-keeper who had played two first-class matches for Warwickshire in 1947, and then became a successful businessman and patron of the game. His business success with Banbury Buildings had allowed him to indulge his sporting passions both in football as chairman of Coventry City and in cricket where he was the organiser of the Eastbourne Festival. In 1969 his team, D.H.Robins' XI, played the opening first-class match against the West Indian tourists at Eastbourne with the 54-year-old Robins as captain of a side containing eight Test players. John Shepherd, in his first match as a member of a West Indies tour party, was in the West Indies team for that match. Shepherd recalls Robins as being cricket-mad, proud, with a giant-sized ego and a rather a steam-rolling approach when any obstacles came in his way!

After South Africa's exclusion from official international cricket post-1970, the South African administrator Jack Cheetham asked Robins if he would organise a private tour to South Africa to take place in early 1973 and Robins agreed. The all-white tour party was captained by David Brown and included other England Test players in John Murray, Robin Hobbs, John Hampshire and Bob Willis, as well as experienced county players like Clive Radley, Roger Knight, Frank Hayes and John Lever. The team was a strong one and they were surprised how fervently competitive the cricket was - notwithstanding that the visitors were part of a private and very unofficial tour. In the final first-class match of the tour there were 17,000 spectators at the Wanderers in Johannesburg for the Saturday of the unofficial 'Test'. As Bob Willis put it, 'The South Africans were very disappointed at being ostracised from Test cricket ... they were very keen to show that they were still a force to be reckoned with'.[80] On the pitch they certainly did that - winning the 'Test' by an innings with a Barry Richards century and major contributions from Eddie Barlow and Mike Procter with the ball.

On 27 September 1973 the news broke that the party for Derrick Robins' next tour of South Africa, scheduled for October to December of that year, would include the Pakistani Younis Ahmed and Kent's John Shepherd. At a dinner in Cape Town the South African Minister of Sport, Piet Koornhof,

79 Peter Hain, *Don't Play with Apartheid*, George Allen and Unwin, 1971.
80 Bob Willis, *The Cricket Revolution*, Sidgwick and Jackson 1981.

had announced that the Government had approved Younis' and Shepherd's inclusion in the side and this was followed by a statement from the President of the (all-white) South African Cricket Association, Boon Wallace, that both players were 'very keen' to come to South Africa and that he was 'delighted ... that the selected team is welcomed' (a clear reference to the D'Oliveira Affair of 1968). The tour party captain was the indomitable Brian Close and he was joined by a high-quality group of English professionals with international experience such as Graham Roope, John Lever, Roger Tolchard and John Snow. Shepherd's county colleagues Graham Johnson and Bob Woolmer were also in the party and the Kent connection was strengthened further as Les Ames was to manage the side.

For the 1973 season Kent had improved the salary of John Shepherd from £1,850 per annum to £2,150 per annum, a rise of 16%, although much of this seemingly generous increase was to be eaten away by inflation which was over 9% in the year. This meant that his salary, at the age of 29, was almost exactly the same as the UK average earnings of £2,170.[81] The younger Bob Woolmer (25) and Graham Johnson (26) were paid £1,750 that year. Whilst these salaries were arguably satisfactory, given the norms of the time, there was always a need to supplement the earnings outside of the cricket season. So for John Shepherd and the other two Kent-contracted professionals the offer, conveyed to them by the appointed tour manager Les Ames, of generous remuneration for some eight weeks of work in South Africa was obviously attractive. The same applied to the other members of the tour party of course – they were all full-time cricket professionals who no doubt reasoned that careers were short and that every opportunity to augment their modest county earnings should be pursued.

The other non-white player on the tour, Surrey's 27-year-old Pakistani batsman Younis Ahmed, put the case clearly at the time:

> There is no mystery why I came on this tour. First of all I am a professional cricketer and I go anywhere in the world where I can earn my living. In this case I was offered £100 per week, plus all expenses, for this eight-week trip with the Derrick Robins XI. And since I have been out here I have signed a further three-month contract to play and coach in Rhodesia ... also at £100 a week plus accommodation, plus car. Where in England could any county cricketer match that sort of payment in an English winter? So as a professional cricketer I just had to take the offers.[82]

In reality of course Younis Ahmed did not 'have to take the offer' any more than John Shepherd or any other member of the touring party **had** to be involved. They **chose** to for the reasons that Younis stated – and John

81 Equivalent to £32,000 in 2009 money.

82 Crawford White, 'Younis, Shepherd beat apartheid', in (London) *Daily Express*, 13 December 1973.

Shepherd today says the same. He was a professional and his main motivation was, like Younis Ahmed's, to secure remunerative winter employment - his attitude was 'Have bat, will travel'. It was a job and he had a family to look after and a mortgage to pay - and times were difficult, with inflation high and rising in response to massive increase in oil prices and the British economy tottering - a three-day week was shortly to be introduced by the Heath Government. His only real concern was to be assured that his decision to go on the tour would not affect his rights as a Barbadian citizen to return to his home country - not necessarily to play cricket there but just to visit. In both Younis' and Shepherd's cases the choice they made meant that they virtually ended their international careers - although Younis did play for Pakistan thirteen years later, having served a ban imposed by the Pakistan Cricket Board. Shepherd was to have no such luck - although, as we have seen, he had in any case been informed that his international career was over a couple of years before he chose to go on the D.H.Robins tour. Indeed Shepherd's decision to go to South Africa was at least in part influenced by what he saw as his rejection by the West Indies.

Shepherd was never quite banned by the West Indies, although he was certainly criticised, even lambasted, by some for the choice that he made. At the beginning of the 1974 county season his Kent colleague and fellow West Indian Bernard Julien, who had been on the 1973 England tour and had also played against England in their 1973/74 visit to the Caribbean, told him that the West Indies captain Rohan Kanhai, when he had heard about Shepherd's decision, had said 'They should ban the black bastard'. Kanhai was to go to South Africa himself later that very year when he played four matches for Transvaal in the Dadabhai Trophy in the 1974/75 season, and within a few years a number of other West Indians were to follow the path that he and John Shepherd had trodden!

Undoubtedly both Younis and Shepherd were being used by the South African cricket authorities, and by Robins, to give a multi-racial veneer to the tour and to lay the trail for what they hoped would be press reports that, in cricket at least, progress was being made towards the breaking down of racial barriers in South African society. This was all part of South African cricket's rather disingenuous PR campaign to try and persuade that a process of normalisation was under way in cricket if not elsewhere. Crawford White's *Daily Express* article at the end of the Robins tour and stories about the removal of 'petty apartheid' laws in other right-of-centre British newspapers like the *Daily Mail*'s 'Apartheid law takes a big knock' and the *Daily Telegraph*'s 'Whites only signs are taken down', in February 1974, were part of this campaign. At the same time, whilst the Robins tours were certainly unofficial, there was at least a tacit acceptance of them by the English cricket establishment. It has been noted that the minute books of the Cricket Council, the governing body of English cricket, '... do not indicate that it tried to discourage the Robins' tours'[83] and no doubt Robins

83 Jack Williams, *Cricket and Race*, Berg, 2001.

and especially the highly respected Les Ames would have also have reported positively back to the authorities at the end of the tour.

On this first tour John Shepherd was an 'honorary white' – a bizarre status which required him to have a minder in the shadows who was there to sort out any situation which might be sensitive. For example, as Shepherd spent 95% of his time in areas that were reserved exclusively for whites, the minder had to smooth the way – with hotel and restaurant staff, and other guests who might question what a 'Kaffir' was doing in one of their exclusive places. This was not just a courtesy to Shepherd, but also a pragmatic necessity in order to keep the tour on track. Had there been an incident in which Shepherd was insulted or abused, and had this got out to the media as it probably would have done, then the tour would have been in jeopardy.

The Robins tour was undoubtedly, as we have seen, a determined attempt by the white South Africa cricket authorities to keep the door open to the rest of the cricketing world and to try and present a more acceptable face to them. At its end Derrick Robins said that the tour 'could do a lot towards re-establishing South Africa-England links in time for the scheduled MCC tour of South Africa in three years time.'[84] This, of course, was to turn out to be wishful thinking and the only cricket visitors for the next seventeen years were those on the private and then rebel tours. The cricketing elements of the 1973 tour were secondary to the public-relations component. That, in truth, was why John Shepherd and Younis Ahmed were in the tour party in the first place and why, for example, they were asked to be in the side which played an 'historic' match against an African XI in Soweto at the beginning of the tour. It was pure PR: window-dressing which could not obscure the racial divide in cricket which, at that time, was as great as the divide in any other part of South African society.[85] With the benefit of hindsight Shepherd today recognises that he and Younis were being used and that their presence on this tour was tokenism. But he still feels, as he said at the time, that he 'made a contribution to good race relations [in South Africa and Rhodesia]' and that his South African connection was 'from my point of view ... a pleasing and enjoyable experience'.[86]

Notwithstanding the real and scarcely disguised reason for the tour, some good cricket was nevertheless played and the tour party acquitted themselves well, losing only one of their thirteen matches. John Shepherd played well throughout the tour. The first of the three 'mini-tests' was at Newlands – the beautiful home of Western Province in Cape Town and hitherto an all-white preserve on the field of play. Shepherd showed his allround skills by taking four wickets in the home side's first innings and

84 Quoted in *Johannesburg Star*, 24 November 1973.

85 A second match against an African XI was arranged for Port Elizabeth but this was abandoned without play because of rain.

86 Quoted in Andre Odendaal, *Cricket in Isolation*, Cape Town, published by its author, 1977.

then scoring a sparkling 30 – he was warmly applauded from every part of the ground as he returned to the pavilion. But for Shepherd the highlight of the tour was in the final match at the Wanderers ground in Johannesburg. The Robins eleven were in trouble at 167 for seven in their first innings when Shep came to the wicket. Then 'mixing sheer hitting with copybook drives and glides [he] slammed 53 out of 60 while he was at the wicket. In just under an hour, he faced 51 balls and hit 5 fours and two magnificent, cross-batted sixes off Procter and Van der Bijl.'[87] Shep had been cheered all the way to the wicket by the overwhelmingly white crowd of 15,000 who stood to applaud him – and he was cheered even more loudly on his return to the pavilion after his fine innings. *Wisden* called it a 'glorious hour at the wicket'. He says today that it was the 'biggest moment of my cricketing life – although I wish that it had happened at Canterbury, Bridgetown or Sabina Park'.

John Shepherd's experiences throughout this tour were, to say the least, very strange for he felt '100% African' as a black South African had so warmly addressed him – before going on to say ' ... I've never met a black Shepherd before. Did you leave your sheep on the pastures of Kent?' In the elite Rand International Hotel in Johannesburg Shepherd went to the kitchens to talk to the staff to try to find out what life was like for them – and he found out that it was pretty horrible. It was no fun to be a black man or woman in John Vorster's racially divided Republic. Shep was the most popular member of the team – waiters had never seen a black man in the dining-room so he got double helpings of steak for breakfast! But the ambivalence of his presence and the uncomfortable likelihood that some in the black community regarded him as a traitor, or at least as an Uncle Tom, came home to him when he visited a non-white, mainly Indian, cricket match in Durban on his own initiative on his day off. At this match he met Pat Naidoo who was legal advisor to the South African Cricket Board of Control, the then governing body for black cricket and strong opponents of any cricket tours from abroad. Shepherd was shocked when Naidoo, who had initially seemed friendly, introduced him to his two sons as 'the man who would rather play with the whites than come and play with us'. Shepherd was to see Naidoo again on future visits and he still regrets that an apology was never forthcoming from him.

John Shepherd's next visit to southern Africa was in September 1974 when he was part of an 'International Wanderers' tour to Rhodesia which also included one match in Johannesburg. This international team, as ever under Brian Close's captaincy, was predominantly English but also included, for some games, the South Africans Eddie Barlow, Peter Carlstein, Graeme Pollock and Barry Richards, the Pakistani Younis Ahmed, the Australians Ian Chappell and Garth McKenzie and the New Zealander Glenn Turner. The organisers congratulated themselves that they had a representative of every Test nation in the party – other than India. It was a provocative visit, although perhaps not intended to be so – and it was not

87 *Johannesburg Star*, 24 November 1973.

the first. Rhodesia had declared independence from Britain unilaterally in 1965 and declared itself to be an independent republic in 1969. However, other than South Africa and Portugal, no country recognised Rhodesia as legitimate and United Nations and other sanctions applied. The Wanderers tour was borderline 'sanctions-busting' – although none of the cricketers realised this at the time. The cricket-related implications of sanctions were limited as Rhodesia was in a cricketing sense a part of South Africa and played as a 'pseudo-province' in South African domestic tournaments. In the past, pre-UDI, English counties had made occasional tours in the country but it was not until 1972 that an overseas team had played in Rhodesia, although, as we have seen, Garry Sobers unwittingly stirred up a huge controversy when he visited and played in the country briefly in 1970. The International Wanderers team, which had visited in September 1972, played only three matches but it included in its party Basil D'Oliveira – the symbolism of his involvement was unlikely to have been missed by supporters of an open approach to cricket in southern Africa around the world! The 1974 tour party played five matches in Rhodesia and one in Johannesburg against Transvaal and won them all. Shepherd played particularly well in the two first-class matches, scoring 30 and 71* and taking two for 56 and four for 37 versus Rhodesia and scoring a first-innings 63* and taking three for 61 and none for 27 versus Transvaal.

John Shepherd in conversation with Rhodesia's Prime Minister, Ian Smith, at the Police Ground in Salisbury in September 1974.
From left to right: Glenn Turner, Tony Greig, Graham Roope, Younis Ahmed, John Shepherd, Eddie Barlow, Mike Harris, Tony Brown, Peter Sainsbury, Jack Simmons, Ian Smith, Roger Tolchard, Janet Smith and Brian Close.

The Rhodesia tour finished in September 1974 and Shepherd was looking for a winter job when Derrick Robins popped up again with an offer for him to join a tour party to the West Indies in October and November. Unsurprisingly this tour was controversial from the start and the planned schedule had to be changed when the governments of Guyana and of Trinidad refused the party entry because of their South African connections. But the tour (which involved no first-class matches) did go ahead, visiting Barbados, Grenada, St Lucia, St Vincent and some of the other small islands including Antigua. Lester Bird, the Prime Minister of Antigua, welcomed them and said that Robins by taking multi-racial teams to South Africa was contributing to the 'breaking down of apartheid': not a remark that played well throughout the Caribbean!

In February 1975 Derrick Robins returned to South Africa, under Brian Close's captaincy and Ken Barrington's management, for the third successive year for an eight-match tour. Once again John Shepherd and Younis Ahmed were in the party which again mainly comprised English county professionals - one of them was Clive Radley who was Shepherd's room-mate. The side won none of its five first-class matches, although Shep himself did well enough, scoring 233 runs at 46.60 and taking 14 wickets at 33.35. It seems that the close company of a minder that Shepherd had 'enjoyed' on his first visit no longer applied and that, although his status was nominally unchanged, life was more difficult. On one occasion Radley and his wife were travelling in a car with Radley driving, his wife in the middle of a bench seat and Shepherd on the outside - it was a bit cramped and Shep had his arm along the top of the seat to make more room. They were observed by an official-looking white man who wanted to know what was going on between the black Shepherd and the white lady next to him.[88] These incidents were few in number but cumulatively they had some effect on Shepherd who tended to spend more time in his room than on his previous South African tour. As had been the case in 1973 the opponents of the Robins XI were mostly all-white teams but they also played one match in Soweto against an 'African XI' and, as a token, two non-white players were included in a one-day President's XI match against the tourists at Newlands.

In September 1975 Shepherd was back in Rhodesia for another short, five-match 'International Wanderers' tour, this time under Glenn Turner's captaincy. Shep played in two of the matches. Prior to the tour he had partnered Geoffrey Greenidge[89] in a double-wicket competition in Johannesburg - the two had formed a strictly unaccredited 'West Indies' team - and Greenidge had become the third West Indian, after Sobers and

88 Mixed-race marriages were prohibited in 1949. Adulterous relationships between whites and non-whites were prohibited by the weirdly-titled Immorality Amendment Act of 1950. The latter was not to be repealed until 1985.

89 Geoffrey Greenidge was a white Barbadian whose participation in this tournament, and in one subsequent International Wanderers match in Salisbury, led to the Guyanese government cancelling a Shell Shield match with Barbados for which he had been selected.

D.H.Robins' XI at Port Elizabeth in March 1975.
Standing (l to r): Clive Radley, Younis Ahmed, Eddie Hemmings, Frank Hayes, Stuart Turner, Max Walker, Steve Rouse, Terry Jenner and Roger Tolchard.
Seated: John Shepherd, John Hampshire, Brian Close (captain), Derrick Robins, Ken Barrington (manager), Don Bennett (coach) and Bruce Francis.
On ground: Malcolm Francke and John Lyon (wk).
Three other members of the side, Geoff Greenidge, Tony Greig and John Steele are absent from this picture.

Shepherd, to play cricket in southern Africa. This competition included two other non-white players - Mohamed Ilyas and Younis Ahmed, who played in defiance of a ban imposed by the Pakistan Cricket Board. A similar ban had been instituted by the cricket boards in India and the West Indies - so in a sense the three non-white participants in this brief tournament were the first cricketing rebels - the first actually to defy instructions from their respective cricketing authorities.

During one of the matches on the 'International Wanderers' tour, in Salisbury, Shepherd was approached by Suman Mehta of the Indian (Hindu) Club and asked whether he would play for one of their members - the Sunrise Sports Club. When news of Shepherd's acceptance of this offer leaked out there was a storm in the media in respect of the possibility that Shep might also play for Rhodesia. The President of the South African Cricket Association, Billy Woodin, said that Shepherd would not be allowed to play as a member of the Rhodesian team in South Africa because of his colour. This statement was eventually contradicted by South Africa's Minister of Sport, Piet Koornhof, and, after a brief return visit to England, Shepherd and his wife flew back to Salisbury to take up the appointment with Sunrise: he was captain and coach as well as senior player. On a personal note, Terry Shepherd was pregnant throughout their stay with their daughter Caroline who was born, back in England, the following May. The Shepherds were provided with a good apartment in the up-market and exclusively white (apart from the servants) Baines Avenue in Salisbury. One day, shortly after they had moved in, Terry was entering the apartment block and the superintendent on duty saw her walking towards the lift and said: 'Excuse me, dear, you are supposed to use the stairs,' a remark that was greeted by Terry (who was a feisty lady and who had been a sympathiser of the Black Power movement when a young woman) with both barrels!

The cricket was multi-racial in that Sunrise, an Indian team, played against other Asian and white teams - although each of the teams was not racially mixed - so John Shepherd was perhaps an 'honorary Indian' when he played for Sunrise! The standard of cricket was not high - Sunrise played in the second division of the Rhodesian Cricket League and not surprisingly Shepherd was the star and these performances became known to the selectors of the Rhodesian team. The rules of the South African competitions, the Currie Cup and the Gillette Cup, allowed only one non-Southern African to play in any one match. For Rhodesia that player was now the English fast bowler Robin Jackman who had been playing in South African domestic cricket for five years - initially for Western Province and latterly for Rhodesia.[90] Jackman was carrying a niggling injury in late November and was out of form and John Shepherd was selected to replace him in the Rhodesian side for a Currie Cup match against Transvaal in Salisbury. He therefore became the first black man to play Currie Cup cricket. His selection was welcomed by Billy Woodin, the South African cricket official who had previously doubted his eligibility, who now said: 'I'm indeed very happy to see he has been selected. I'm sure that he'll add a lot of colour and excitement to the Currie Cup.'[91] Shepherd's selection was also marked by an offer of sponsorship from Shell Rhodesia.[92] He performed well in this first match, scoring a bright half-century, having been given a standing ovation by the crowd as he came out to bat. The innings characteristically included a huge six which Shep 'smashed with immense power over the commentary box for the biggest six I have seen at this ground'.[93] He also bowled economically in Transvaal's first innings. When Transvaal batted again Shepherd came on first change and, in conditions which were ideal for his style, got the ball to swing prodigiously and bowled 13 overs for only 12 runs. The formidable Transvaal batsmen Clive Rice and Norman Featherstone began to restore the innings but the Rhodesian captain, Brian Davison, failed to throw the ball to Shepherd for another spell - much to Shepherd's surprise - even when the batsmen reach a partnership of over 150! Today Shepherd believes that Davison was probably acting under orders not to allow him to bowl in case he took a

---

90 In that 1975/76 domestic South Africa season other English players included Fred Titmus, Bob Woolmer and Phil Edmonds.

91 Reported in the *Rhodesia Herald*, November 1975. (The cutting is undated.)

92 Shell Rhodesia offered Shepherd up to $100 per match on the condition that he made no public mention of the offer. This was because Shell was allegedly involved in determined sanctions-busting operations to keep oil flowing to the rebel country and did not want to draw any attention to itself at all at the time. Shep got his $100 for each match!

93 Glen Byron in the *Rhodesia Herald*, 30 November 1975.

hatful of wickets and the selectors would then have been forced to pick him for Rhodesia's next Currie Cup matches, which were to be in Cape Town and Port Elizabeth in early December!

When the party for the two matches in South Africa was announced Shepherd was indeed not in it, his place being taken by the out-of-form Jackman. John Shepherd smelled a rat. He realised that had he gone with the Rhodesian team he would again have to have been designated an 'honorary white' in South Africa where apartheid was still very much alive and ill – which would have been unprecedented and very complex for all involved. There was also the point that the Rhodesian cricketers took advantage of their tours to South Africa to stock up on all the goods that were not, because of sanctions, for sale in Rhodesia so, if Shepherd had taken Jackman's place, the latter would have missed out on that perk! The normally mild-mannered Shepherd for once blew his top as he became aware of all of these shenanigans saying that he was 'bloody angry' and said that 'If I was offered $10,000 I would never play for Rhodesia again. I feel that I have been used.' This remark was, of course, immediately picked up by the press.[94] The president of the Rhodesian Cricket Union, David Lewis, then announced that Shepherd had not been selected only for 'cricket reasons' (shades of D'Oliveira!) and that Robin Jackman was preferred because he ' ... always bowled well at sea level'! Immediately after this furore broke in the press Barry Richards, the Natal captain and an icon of South African cricket, issued a statement in which he said that it was ' ... obvious that Shepherd's colour has influenced the decision. ... I am damn sure that if someone else – a player of a different colour – had put up as tremendous a showing as Shepherd did at the weekend he would not have been left out.'[95] Many in Rhodesia agreed, accusing the selectors as having originally pandered to the South African Cricket Board and calling for their resignations. This was heady stuff and the legitimacy of John Shepherd's case, and of Barry Richards' suspicions, was strengthened when Jackman, bowling at sea level at Newlands, failed to take a wicket and conceded 83 runs in 26 overs the following week against Western Province as Rhodesia fell to an innings defeat.

Back in Rhodesia events were taking an extraordinary turn. An article had appeared in the *Zimbabwe Star*, the weekly newspaper of the African National Congress headed by Joshua Nkomo, who was also the founder of the of the Zimbabwe African People's Union and a leader of the armed struggle against the white Rhodesia government. This article has reported that ' ... by coming to Rhodesia Shepherd betrayed the cause of blacks ... his selection for Rhodesia merely reinforces the white people's belief that there is nothing wrong with their society'.[96] Shortly after this article appeared John Shepherd was summoned to Meikles Hotel in Salisbury to

94 This and the following quotations from David Lewis were reported in 'Reaction as Rhodesia drop Shepherd', *The Times*, 3 December 1975.
95 'Colour blamed for dropping of Shepherd', *The Times*, 4 December 1975
96 Reported in the *Sunday Mail*, 14 December 1975.

meet Nkomo. Shepherd was understandably concerned when this giant of a man, with an unrivalled reputation in Rhodesia for defending the rights of the black man, entered the room. 'I'm in real trouble now,' Shep thought. He need not have been worried. Nkomo offered his huge hand and shook Shepherd's warmly: 'Mr Shepherd, I just want to welcome you to Rhodesia', he said in a very softly spoken voice, 'and I do apologise for the article in the newspaper – I did not sanction it.'

Whilst Rhodesia did not formally practice apartheid there was in reality a significant racial divide as in South Africa – which John Shepherd and his wife were soon to realise. Shortly after the 'non-selection' incident Shepherd and his wife were invited for a lunch by his patron the Asian Suman Mehta who, it transpired, had also been a freedom fighter and had been imprisoned with Nkomo. The white waiter ignored them in the restaurant and when Mehta later phoned the restaurant owner to complain, he said that he was sorry because his 'stupid waiter hadn't realised that it was John Shepherd' – *i.e.* that Shep was a famous honorary white!

The Rhodesia side, after their humiliation at Newlands, had moved on to play Eastern Province in Port Elizabeth where they fared better in a drawn match, but with Robin Jackman again wicketless. Currie Cup matches against Transvaal (which was won, with Jackman back in the wickets) and Natal (lost by 10 wickets) followed. By then the issue of John Shepherd's non-selection had rumbled on in South Africa, not least because of Barry Richards' criticism, and eventually the Rhodesian selectors relented and chose Shepherd for the next match – a one-day Gillette Cup game against Eastern Province in Port Elizabeth on 31 January 1976. On arrival at his hotel in Port Elizabeth Shepherd saw Brian Davison the Rhodesian captain who greeted him with the words, 'You got the money then!' – a reference to Shep's remark that he wouldn't play for $10,000. Shepherd's first reaction to this frosty greeting was to think that he should get the next plane back to Salisbury but he played – and then, back in Rhodesia again, he played twice more in Currie Cup matches. Shepherd helped Rhodesia get the better of a draw with Western Province in Salisbury, with innings of 65 and 33 and bowling of three for 34 and one for 27, and he also played his part in a win against Eastern Province at Bulawayo.

John Shepherd's final visit to South Africa came immediately after the completion of his contract with the Salisbury club, Sunrise. The Australian Test cricketer turned commentator Richie Benaud managed a strong side, captained by Greg Chappell and which included most of the Australian bowling attack which had recently played so well in the Australians' 5-1 series drubbing of the West Indies in Australia. It was a seven-match tour in March and April 1976 and along with Shepherd in the party were his Kent colleagues Derek Underwood and Mike Denness. The tour was highly political with the various racially-structured factions of South African cricket battling one another both before and during the matches. There is no doubt that the tourists and the South African cricketers themselves thought that the inclusion of non-white players in all of the 'home' teams and declarations about the new bias for multi-racial cricket would herald in a fresh epoch in South African cricket. A statement was issued by the South African captain Eddie Barlow during the final match which said as much:

> The [South African] players ... want to express their feelings of enthusiasm and honour at having been part of a new era in South African cricket ... the games have shown that cricket knows no barriers and that the way is now open for South African cricket to be normalised as soon as possible.[97]

It was, of course, not to be and whilst no doubt Benaud and the other participants in the tour were sincere in their hopes that it might be a watershed, and Barlow and the rest of the South African players were convinced that very real progress was being made, South African cricket was to have to wait another sixteen years before formally being welcomed back into the international cricket community. But no doubt unknown to Barlow and the rest, the institutionalised racism in the society was experienced in its starkest by their honorary white John Shepherd. Derek Underwood picks up the story: 'A group of us were in a bar in a hotel in Durban and John was refused service by the barman when it was his turn to buy a round. I didn't know how to handle it. John was furious and I was also very upset about it.' Mike Denness also recalls the incident: 'It was a serious problem which I brought to the attention of Richie Benaud who ensured that the culpable barman was dismissed by the hotel management'.[98]

Shepherd acquitted himself well on the tour - the highlight being his dismissal of Richards, Pollock and Irvine as the South Africans slipped to 86 for six in their first innings in the last 'mini-Test' at Durban.

In May 1976 the West Indies Cricket Board of Control (WICBC) issued an unequivocal statement. They said that

> ... all players from Caribbean territories under its jurisdiction who play cricket or coach in South Africa or Rhodesia will not be permitted to participate in matches organised under the auspices of the Board at home or abroad. In addition, the Board reaffirms that no official team from any country which tours South Africa or Rhodesia will be welcome in the West Indies...[99]

In June 1976 the focus of the world's attention was on South Africa when on the sixteenth of that month more than 200 black people were killed and countless hundreds injured when police opened fire on young protestors in Soweto. For those observers overseas, still in ignorance about apartheid and oppression in South Africa, these shocking events were an eye-opener - and for those who argued against playing sport in South Africa, or against

97 Quoted in Andre Odendaal, *Cricket in Isolation*, Cape Town, published by its author, 1977.

98 Interviews with the author, October 2008.

99 Quoted in Hilary Beckles, *The Development of West Indies Cricket: The Age of Nationalism*, Pluto Press, 1998.

South African teams, they were a tragic justification. Barely believably, however, the New Zealand rugby authorities pressed ahead with an All Blacks tour in South Africa which began only a couple of weeks after Soweto. This decision led to the boycotting of the Montreal Olympic Games in July by African nations and a year later to the signing of the Gleneagles Agreement which was unanimously approved by Commonwealth presidents and prime ministers, who agreed, as part of their support for the international campaign against apartheid, to 'discourage contact and competition between their sportsmen and sporting organisations, teams or individuals from South Africa'.

In South Africa this tightening of bans against sporting contacts was received with dismay by the cricketing authorities who claimed, with some justification, that whilst the state remained an apartheid state, in cricket real progress towards racial integration was being made. There were many, as we have seen, in the world of cricket outside the Republic who agreed with them. But for John Shepherd there was some relief that the unequivocal statement of the West Indies Board in May and the subsequent Gleneagles agreement made his own position clear - what had been a difficult personal period was now over. He genuinely believed that he should be free to pursue his profession so long as he was within the law and that, as he said at the time, 'I made a contribution to cricket and good race relations ... I have perhaps changed a few narrow views and helped people realise that there is nothing abnormal about playing and mixing with a black person.'[100] His views were echoed in a letter sent by the Chairman of the Bulawayo Sports Club, Mr D.K.Naik, to the West Indian Cricket Board of Control on 29 June 1976. 'Players like John Shepherd,' wrote Mr Naik, ' ... have done a great deal for cricket in South Africa for its own sake as well as to break the immoral discriminatory practices in sport here.'

This is not quite the end of the John Shepherd and South Africa story. The Gleneagles Agreement remained honoured for the rest of the decade and not even Derrick Robins or Richie Benaud were in a position to organise private tours to the republic. But in 1981 the New Zealand rugby authorities invited the South African team to tour New Zealand and, despite protests, the tour went ahead - it was the first 'official' sporting contact between South Africa and the outside world for five years. Perhaps emboldened by this, very secret planning was under way for an unofficial 'England' cricket tour of South Africa to take place in March 1982. In the event the South African Breweries' English XI arrived in the Republic and played eight matches - it was the first 'rebel' tour. The team was captained by Graham Gooch and included John Shepherd's erstwhile Kent colleagues Alan Knott, Derek Underwood and Bob Woolmer. They were handsomely

100 Quoted by Andre Odendaal in *Cricket in Isolation*, published by its author, 1977.

rewarded[101] for their month's work – but banned from international cricket for three years by the England cricket authorities.

In August 1982 John Shepherd was contacted by Bev Walker, of Limelight Management, a sports agent based in England, to ask whether he would be interested in being 'manager/player' on a planned rebel West Indies tour to South Africa to take place in early 1983. The suggestion was that this offer was a sort of belated 'thank you' to Shepherd from the South African cricketing authorities for his involvement in the first series of private tours to South Africa between 1973 and 1976. Shepherd asked who would be going on the tour and was told that such players as Gordon Greenidge, Colin Croft, and others were in the frame. Shepherd was suspicious of this as he knew that all of the players named were currently active in West Indies cricket in the Test or one-day sides and he was, of course, also aware of the fatal consequences for their careers if they were to go on a rebel tour.

Back in Barbados the story broke that a 'rebel' West Indies tour would soon be going to South Africa and that John Shepherd would be the manager. The London *Daily Mail* then reported that the series had been planned but fallen through because the West Indian players had asked too much. An article by Ian Wooldridge said that 16 players ' ... including Colin Croft, Wayne Daniel, Alvin Kallicharran, Sylvester Clarke, Desmond Haynes, Hartley Alleyne, Collis King and John Shepherd, had agreed to play matches in South Africa in January and February 1983 for £130,000 a man'[102] – a sum, he reported, 'that had been rejected by the South African Breweries sponsor.' Shepherd's friend Joel Garner then phoned him to ask what was going on and to tell him that there was a big splash in the Bridgetown press that Shepherd was involved in organising a tour and recruiting players. Shepherd assured him that none of this was true. Shortly afterwards he was attending a reception in London at the Barbados High Commission in connection with a visit by a group of Barbados professional cricketers who were going to be playing a match at The Oval – an annual fixture. He had also been invited to play in the match, but was now told by those organising it that his services were not required – a response to the rumours from Barbados and an action that led Garry Sobers to say 'if you don't play I'm not playing'. It was all highly charged and political! In the end Shepherd didn't play at The Oval but the offer to him firmly materialised when he received a contract from Bev Walker. The offer spelled out in the contract was extremely generous. In return for a little over one month's work he would be paid £50,000[103] and there would be another tour in 1983 of similar duration for which he would be paid ' ... not less than £55,000'. John Shepherd turned down this offer and looking back today, from the perspective of more than twenty-five years later, he is glad that he did. As a younger man, from 1973 to 1976, he had taken a

101 Bob Woolmer revealed in his autobiography, *Pirate and Rebel?*, published in 1984, that he was paid £10,000. *Wisden* 1983 recorded that the scale of remuneration was £10,000 to £40,000.

102 Reported by Reg Hayter in *The Cricketer*, October 1982.

103 Roughly seven times his annual salary at Gloucestershire at the time.

different decision, but by 1982 not only were the times different but the sanctions that would have been placed on him and the censure that would have followed in his home country would not have made it worth it - even for that much money.[104]

The story of the world of cricket's involvement with South Africa in the years between the D'Oliveira affair in 1968 and South Africa's return to international cricket in 1991 is complex and even today it is a source of differences of opinion. The quote from the *Wisden* anthology at the head of this chapter surely summarises it well. It is fair to say that, like *Wisden*, few cricketers, cricket administrators, cricket-loving public figures or even journalists saw at the time that C.L.R.James' famous question 'What do they know of cricket who only cricket know?' should have applied unequivocally in any analysis of South Africa in the 1970s and 1980s. The exceptions, John Arlott, Mike Brearley and the Rev David Sheppard amongst them, had the moral high ground at the time and hindsight has proved them to be right. And Peter Hain, the *bête noire* of the establishment back in 1970, was right as well when he said about apartheid: ' ... if you do not resolutely oppose it, then you support it ... '. But back in 1973, John Shepherd was surrounded not by those who could see the relevance and moral authority of the Jamesian maxim, nor by his Bajan peers and potential sources of advice back home in Barbados. Shep was playing for Kent where his mentors were Les Ames and Colin Cowdrey whose firm convictions were clear from Cowdrey's later comment about the 1973 Robins tour: 'I applaud [Robins'] zeal in trying to maintain cricket links with South Africa.'[105] Furthermore Cowdrey said that on this tour John Shepherd and Younis Ahmed ' ... were accorded the normal courtesies and were well received'. Ames said on his return from the tour:

> We experienced no apartheid problems at all. There were no protests or demonstrations, and the whole tour went very well indeed. Shepherd proved the most popular player in the side. Both he and Younis got wonderful receptions wherever they went, but Shepherd especially so ... we played multi-racial cricket on our side against teams who were all white, all black or all cape coloured.[106]

The improbability, indeed impossibility, of the South African authorities **not** extending the 'normal courtesies' to John Shepherd (*i.e.* by **not** making him an honorary white) and the hypocrisy of all this seems not to have occurred to Cowdrey. Similarly the irony of the fact that whilst the Robins team was 'multi-racial' the teams that they played against were not seems not to have been apparent to Ames! Today John Shepherd does not feel that Ames, Cowdrey and Co deliberately misled him - but he acknowledges

---

104 The rebel West Indies tour went ahead in January and February 1983. A below strength side, under Lawrence Rowe's captaincy, played twelve matches - the seventeen players involved received life bans - which were rescinded in 1989.

105 Colin Cowdrey, *M.C.C.: The Autobiography of a Cricketer*, Hodder and Stoughton, 1976.

106 Interview with John Evans in *Kent Messenger*, 28 December 1973.

that he was useful to them in the pursuit of their goal to maintain cricketing ties with South Africa.

John Shepherd's honest and well-intentioned, if perhaps rather naïve, visits to South Africa were castigated at the time by the anti-apartheid movement, some members of which branded him as a 'traitor to the black cause'[107] - although there was little of such criticism back home in Barbados. For Shepherd personally, he rapidly became aware of the huge disparity in way of life and opportunity between the whites on one side and the rest on the other. He was also shocked that when the South African hosts relaxed their protective grip a bit he was as vulnerable to abuse as any other black man - the incident in the Durban hotel bar was not the only one. It was also the case that some of his fellow tourists were less than sympathetic to the plight of the black South African underclass - he recalls how some of them couldn't wait to get out of Soweto and back to the segregated comforts of their fine hotel.

That any possibility of John Shepherd's recall to the West Indies colours was scuppered by his decision to play in southern Africa is certainly true. But with the passing of time many may now feel that whilst Shep made a mistake to listen too respectfully to the advice of those such as Robins, Cowdrey and Ames who were certainly not without wider agendas,[108] he should not be harshly judged. And for his principled and altruistic decision to have nothing to do with the West Indies rebel tour of 1983 he should be roundly praised.

107 Hilary Beckles, *The Development of West Indies Cricket: The Age of Nationalism*, Pluto Press, 1998.

108 Peter Oborne captures the ambiguity of Cowdrey well when he says that '... Cowdrey was dangerous to take at face value' in *Basil D'Oliveira. Cricket and Conspiracy the Untold Story*, Little Brown, 2004.

Chapter Six
The Consummate Professional

In a season in which all-round team work counted for so much, it was still very justifiable to pick out one man who did so much - and that was the West Indian all-rounder Shepherd. He got useful runs at the right time - he virtually batted Middlesex on his own in the Gillette Cup, hitting a magnificent century - but his seam bowling will be remembered most in 1977. How he bowled - so well and for such long spells throughout the summer. In one match he sent down 77 overs and in eight other games he bowled more than 40 overs in a match. On six occasions he took five wickets in an innings and surely would have crowned such a fine season by taking 100 wickets had it not been for a dreadful rain-soaked spell in August.

Dudley Moore, Wisden Cricketers' Almanack, 1978

At the end of the 1973 season keen cricketer, Kent fan and journalist Dennis Fowle edited and published a 68-page booklet entitled *Kent: The Glory Years*[109] which covered the county's great run from 1967 to 1973 and celebrated the five trophies they had gathered along the way. As we have seen, other than in 1969, when he was on international duty, John Shepherd hardly missed a game over these seven seasons and by 1974 he was in many respects Kent's most valuable player. In seven years of first-class cricket he had scored more than five thousand runs and taken five hundred wickets - not to mention 156 catches. On top of that he was well established as a key performer in the one-day game, nearly always bowling his full allocation of overs and with a handy knack for taking wickets at crucial times. His legendary reliability, both physical and mental, was a source of comfort to coaches and captains who could turn their attention to the flakier members of their squads!

1974

For the 1974 season Kent had every hope that the 'glory' would continue and clearly Shepherd would be a key element in the realising of this ambition. The county had players who had greater individual talent in one part of their game: these were Cowdrey, who was to top the batting averages; Denness and Underwood, who were ever-present in the England side that summer; Asif Iqbal, when available. Only the fast-improving Bob

109 Denis Fowle (ed), *Kent: The Glory Years*, Everest Books, 1974.

Woolmer was to be any rival for John Shepherd's all round skills. Mike Denness recalls how valuable it was for him as captain to have the predominantly swing-bowling Shepherd performing in tandem with the seamer Woolmer - especially in the limited-overs game. Denness tells how the two of them sowed seeds of doubt in the minds of the batsmen with their contrasting styles. He also recalls how Shepherd would be able to bowl shorter or longer spells as was required - and that he never seemed to need much warming up, and hardly ever bowled a 'loosener'. Mike Denness, who captained Shepherd in nearly 250 matches for Kent between 1969 and 1976, saw him as an attacking not a defensive bowler - especially in the three-day game - and says that, because of his allround skills, his fitness and his absolute reliability Shepherd's name would always be one of the first on the team sheet during what were Kent's glory years .[110] In the dressing room Shepherd was also a quiet source of advice and sometimes comfort - to the younger players especially.

Mike Denness had now been captain of Kent for two full seasons and had already put three trophies in the cabinet - and one or two misses as well. Expectations for 1974 were understandably high - the standard set in the 'glory years' was such that to win one of the four county competitions was no more than the norm and, especially for the cricket traditionalists who were still unsure of the true merits of one-day cricket, nothing less than a top-four finish in the County Championship (achieved in four successive years from 1970 to 1973) would do. In the event the purists were to be disappointed as Kent fell to tenth in the three-day competition, but there was another trophy to be celebrated as the Gillette Cup returned to the county for the first time in seven years.

For John Shepherd, returned from his first tour in South Africa, 1974 was a relatively quiet year albeit one with no let-up in his workload. He played in all but two of Kent's twenty County Championship matches, all five of the games in their successful Gillette Cup run, all five of the B&H matches and all sixteen games in the Sunday League. He played 52 innings, scoring 914 runs and bowled 859 overs, taking 89 wickets in all competitions. The bowling burden was all the greater as strike bowler Bernard Julien missed much of the season through injury and Shepherd often had to open the bowling, which was not always the ideal use of his talent. Highlights included the two occasions when he took six wickets in an innings in the Championship - against Glamorgan at Maidstone (six for 42) and against Warwickshire at Canterbury (six for 67). The Glamorgan match was a reduced, one-innings contest, won by Kent when Shep and Bob Woolmer, with Underwood away on international duty, exploited a green wicket to dismiss their opponents for 97. Against Warwickshire in August during Canterbury week the first-day strip was also green and damp and Shepherd, bowling 33 overs unchanged, and Woolmer again prospered with Warwickshire being shot out for 146.

110 Interview with the author, 16 October 2008.

In June Shepherd had a remarkable allround four days at Trent Bridge. In Kent's first innings in the Championship match he and Alan Ealham had a century partnership to rescue the county from 67 for six, with Shepherd going on to score 79 – his highest score of the season. Then, on the second day, when Nottinghamshire batted, and with Woolmer injured, he completed a phenomenal 46 overs, out of 103, taking three wickets for 95. In between these two performances he played in a Sunday League game, helping Kent to a win with one for 36 in 8 overs and then scoring the winning runs, in a brief partnership with Cowdrey, to see Kent home. It was four days of intense and unbroken cricket during which Shepherd bowled 67.3 overs and scored 125 runs.

For Kent the triumph of the season came in the Gillette Cup with comfortable wins against Buckinghamshire, Durham and Leicestershire leading to a semi-final against Somerset at Canterbury in front of a crowd of 15,000. This was a nervier affair notable for the performance of a young eighteen-year-old Somerset cricketer described by John Woodcock as having 'bowled, fielded and batted with any amount of promise'. His name was I.T.Botham and he was batting with confidence when John Shepherd managed to get him caught behind for 19. Then, when Kent chased Somerset's modest total of 154, Botham with his first ball clean bowled a 'pensive' Colin Cowdrey for eight and got his revenge on Shepherd, having him caught 'at cover point by Burgess with his hands in front of his face'.[111] Kent scraped through to the final – and in the years to come the world was to hear quite a bit more of the tyro Botham.

It had been a cold and wet summer and it was no surprise when the Gillette Cup final between Kent and Lancashire was rained off on its planned Saturday date. Winds and some sun on the Sunday meant that play could take place on the Monday and Kent won another close game – although they struggled a bit, losing six wickets chasing a modest target of 119 for victory, with John Shepherd top-scoring with 19. Lancashire had been dismissed on a 'churlish' pitch – the highlight being Kent's spectacular out-cricket, especially the run-outs of Clive Lloyd and David Hughes. The latter fell to a throw from John Shepherd, fielding at long leg, which hit the stumps and which reminded John Woodcock of Learie Constantine in his prime'.[112]

During the winter of 1974/75 John Shepherd was in Rhodesia with the International Wanderers, the West Indies with D.H.Robins' XI and then in South Africa with Derrick Robins again (see Chapter Five). Over the same months Shep's county captain Mike Denness was captaining England in a torrid and unsuccessful Ashes tour in Australia – along with his Kent teammates, Knott, Underwood, Luckhurst ... and Cowdrey who had flown out, at the age of nearly 42 for his sixth tour, as a replacement batsman.

111 John Woodcock, *The Times*, 15 August 1974.
112 John Woodcock, *The Times*, 10 September 1974.

1975

The Kent dressing room at the beginning of the 1975 season was something of a recovery ward for the Aussie-bashed warriors: the Test-experienced contingent was to be increased further by the end of the season after Bob Woolmer made his debut against Australia. In September Kent played Surrey with nine Test cricketers in their side (Luckhurst, Asif Iqbal, Woolmer, Denness, Julien, Cowdrey, Shepherd, Knott and Underwood). But, as in 1974, whilst there was ample batting strength the bowling was again to rely heavily on John Shepherd who bowled more overs than anyone else both in first-class and in one-day matches. Over the season as a whole, in all matches, Shep bowled in 55 of Kent's opponents' innings and, remarkably, took wickets in all but 18 of them. For Kent the season was to be a disappointment with, for the first time since 1971, moderate performances by their high standards in each of the leagues – fifth in the Championship and third in the Sunday League – and early dismissals from both of the knock-out tournaments.

One of the more remarkable matches of John Shepherd's career took place on 17 and 19 May 1975 at Lord's against Middlesex. In a Benson and Hedges group match that was interrupted and delayed by rain Kent, batting first on a treacherous wicket, slumped to 53 for eight when Derek Underwood joined Shepherd at the wicket. Together they eked out another 81 runs of which Underwood's contribution to the record[113] ninth-wicket partnership was 10. When Shep was finally out, caught at wide mid-on in the last of the 55 overs, he had reached 96, which was 70% of Kent's final meagre total of 137. Alan Gibson in *The Times* recorded that one of Shepherd's sixes ' ... nearly knocked down the scoreboard over the grandstand, although this was accidental rather than deliberate, as it should be in a well-ordered cricket society'.[114]. Then, when Middlesex batted, Shepherd not only took three for 21 in eleven overs but also broke a partnership of 89 between Barlow and Featherstone which had seemed to be winning the match for Middlesex – Shepherd dismissed both of them. Derek Underwood remembers this as a match which 'Shep took by the scruff of the neck, shook it and turned it 180 degrees around'.[115] Shepherd was made 'Man of the Match' for the first time in his career.

One of the great social features of Kent cricket has always been the 'weeks' of cricket at Tunbridge Wells, Canterbury and Maidstone, when the grounds surrounded by white marquees take on a blissfully English ambience – especially if blessed with fine weather. In 1975 the Maidstone week in mid-June was so blessed but Kent were without six key players (Asif Iqbal, Julien, Denness, Knott, Underwood, and Woolmer) who were on World Cup duty with their respective countries. Perhaps it was the feeling that if things had worked out differently with the West Indies he would

---

113 This remains the Kent record for the ninth wicket in all limited-overs matches (of which there had been 885 by the end of the 2008 season).

114 *The Times*, 20 May 1975.

115 Interview with the author, 24 September 2008.

SCORE CARD 5p

*Captain +Wicketkeeper

MAIDSTONE JUNE 14th, 16th, 17th, 1975

KENT v. SUSSEX

Hours of Play : 11.00 - 6.30 p.m. 11.00 - 6.30 p.m. 11.00 - 5.30 or 6 p.m.

Intervals : Lunch 1.15 p.m. Tea 4.15 p.m.

Umpires: W. E. Phillipson and P. Rochford Scorers: C. Lewis and W. Denman

Sussex won toss & elected to bat

KENT WON

SUSSEX

	1st Innings		2nd Innings	
1	J R Barclay c Johnson b Graham	15	c Topley b Shepherd	13
2	G A Greenidge c Cowdrey b Shepherd..	25	c Cowdrey b Shepherd ...	0
3	M J Faber c Rowe b Shepherd	5	c Nicholls b Shepherd ..	24
*4	P J Graves c Jarvis b Shepherd	33	c Cowdrey b Shepherd ...	35
5	A E Parsons lbw b Shepherd	34	c Nicholls b Hills	25
6	J J Groome lbw b Shepherd	2	c Nicholls b Hills	5
+7	A W Mansell c Topley b Shepherd	11	c Topley b Shepherd	4
8	C E Waller c Johnson b Jarvis	1	b Shepherd	0
9	J Spencer not out	16	not out	6
10	C Phillipson lbw b Shepherd	0	c Nicholls b Hills	5
11	R P Marshall c Johnson b Shepherd ..	32	b Shepherd	3
	Bs 2 Lb 6 Wd 1 Nb 1	10	Bs 9 Lb 5 Nb 1	15
	TOTAL	184	TOTAL	135

Runs at fall of wicket:

1st Innings: 1-26 2-35 3-80 4-91 5-101 6-127 7-128 8-132 9-137 10-184

2nd Innings: 1-0 2-37 3-38 4-71 5-101 6-110 7-110 8-116 9-129 10-135

Bowling Analysis:

	O	M	R	W	Wd	Nb	O	M	R	W	Nb
Shepherd	32.5	6	93	8		1	39	11	54	7	1
Graham	20	3	56	1			-	-	-	-	
Jarvis	12	3	25	1	1		10	4	26	0	
Hills	-	-	-	-			19.5	4	40	3	

KENT

1st Innings

*1	B W Luckhurst c Mansell b Spencer ..	26
2	G W Johnson lbw b Spencer	89
3	M C Cowdrey c Waller b Marshall	10
4	A G Ealham run out	25
+5	D Nicholls c Mansell b Phillipson ..	68
6	J N Shepherd c Graves b Barclay	52
7	C Rowe c Phillipson b Barclay	25
8	R Hills c Faber b Barclay	4
9	P Topley c Mansell b Spencer	19
10	J N Graham not out	0
11	K Jarvis lbw b Spencer	0
	Bs 5 Lb 5 Wd 1	11
	TOTAL	329

Runs at fall of wicket:

1st Innings: 1-79 2-107 3-139 4-160 5-171 6-293 7-305 8-329 9-329 10-329

Bowling Analysis:

	O	M	R	W	Wd
Spencer	37	5	99	4	
Marshall	30	8	94	1	
Waller	23	8	46	0	
Phillipson	25	7	58	1	1
Barclay	12.2	7	21	3	

HOST: (Sat.) W. E. Rice, Esq., C.B.E., J.P. J. W. Boddington, Esq.

NEXT HOME MATCH: June 25th, 26th and 27th : v. AUSTRALIANS at CANTERBURY

June 15th v. WORCESTERSHIRE at CANTERBURY (John Player League)

MEMBERSHIP—Join the K.C.C.C., details can be obtained from the office on the ground.

The Kent County Cricket Annual is available on the ground, Price 25p.

Scorecard showing John Shepherd's fifteen-wicket match return - his best in first-class cricket. (In the Sussex second innings, Shepherd bowled 29 overs, not 39 as shown.)

have been with them that inspired Shepherd, for his feats that glorious Maidstone week were prodigious. In the first of the two County Championship matches, against Worcestershire, he took four for 55 in the opponents' second innings to dismiss them for 183 and set up a run chase - 187 to win. Then, with Kent floundering a bit at 129 for seven, Shep guided them home with a fine 53* for a two-wicket victory. In the second match, against Sussex, Shepherd opened the bowling and in an unchanged spell of 32.5 overs, took eight for 93. He followed this by scoring 52, helping Kent to recover from 171 for five to post a solid 329. Shep opened the bowling again in Sussex's second innings and in another unchanged spell of 29 overs he took seven for 54 and Kent won the match by an innings and 10 runs. *Wisden* hailed 'a magnificent all-round performance' and recorded that Shepherd's match figures of 15 for 147 were the first fifteen-wicket haul by a Kent bowler for sixteen years. This was to be John Shepherd's best match analysis in first-class cricket. In June he played his part in Kent's epic win against the Australians, their first for 76 years and a match highlighted by Colin Cowdrey's penultimate first-class century in his final year with Kent - a chanceless 151*. In the county's following match Shepherd set up a good win over Lancashire by taking four quick wickets for seventeen runs in 10.5 overs (24-10-59-5 in total) with 'late movement off the pitch'[116] to reduce their opponents to 45 for four in their second innings and, eventually, to 166 all out. Kent, who had been in the lower reaches of the Championship table only a few weeks before, were now fourth. Two more wins in the next matches against Northamptonshire and Nottinghamshire took the county, by mid-July, to second place just one point behind Lancashire and hopes were rising that a first County Championship for five years could be won - but it was not to be as the county only won two of their remaining nine matches and finished a respectable but disappointing fifth. There was disappointment as well in the one-day competitions with early exits from the two knock-out tournaments and occasional vulnerability in the Sunday League which turned a table-topping position in mid August into an eventual third place. Between 1970 and 1978 Kent only had two seasons in which they failed to win a tournament - 1971 and 1975 (a disappointment for the county President, Les Ames, that there were no trophies in his year of office). For John Shepherd it was a hard season and, unusually, he missed a few of matches with niggling injuries. Despite this his bowling workload was down only a little from previous years and he still bowled more overs than any other Kent bowler in both the Championship and the one-day matches. Shepherd was the leading wicket-taker in the Sunday League and second behind Underwood in first-class matches. His batting was rarely crucial as Kent had such a powerful batting line-up, even when some players were away on Test duty, but there were a number of classic Shep innings - not least his first century in the County Championship for five years batting up the order at No.5 against Middlesex at Canterbury in August, albeit in a losing cause. This innings of 116, with 3 sixes and 11 fours, was

116 John Woodcock in *The Times*, 2 July 1975.

enthusiastically described by *The Times* as being 'defiant ... hard hitting ... splendidly aggressive' and full of 'thrilling' and 'inventive' strokes.[117]

Less than two weeks after the end of the English domestic season John Shepherd was en route to Southern Africa for his final tours of Rhodesia and South Africa and his brief and headline-grabbing spell with the Rhodesian Currie Cup side (see Chapter Five).

1976

A county as accustomed to success as Kent now was could not be satisfied with the meagre returns of 1975: 'extremely disappointing' was Les Ames' rather mournful descriptor in his president's report in the 1976 Kent annual. So when the players gathered for the new season, Mike Denness' fifth and controversially, his last as captain, there was hope for better things and a return to trophy-winning ways. In many respects 1976 was the end of an era – and not just at Kent with stalwarts of the past like Denness, Luckhurst, Cowdrey and Graham making their final appearances for the County. The world of cricket was mostly calm during this long, hot summer – Tony Greig failed to make the West Indies 'grovel' as he had promised and England were comfortably beaten in the Test series – although Kent's Knott, Woolmer and Underwood were far from disgraced as ever-presents in the England side. But unknown to the cricketing authorities, a storm was brewing down-under as a hitherto little-known Australian, Kerry Packer, was quietly plotting an audacious coup that would change the game forever. But that was a year away as John Shepherd and his colleagues reported for duty in April 1976. The following month, on 31 May, John's wife Terry gave birth to a daughter they named Caroline.

Whilst the formidable West Indies team revelled in the near-Caribbean conditions of a summer of almost unbroken sunshine, their compatriot, new father John Shepherd also found things very much to his liking with the bat, finishing third in both the Kent first-class and one-day averages and scoring 1,355 runs with ten half-centuries in all competitions. His bowling workload was slightly down from 1975 as once again a few matches were missed mid-season with back problems and he also missed most of the end of the season games after he suffered a broken jaw when he was hit by the Leicestershire medium-pacer Paddy Clift in the second innings of a Championship match at Grace Road. *Wisden*'s almost annual tribute to Shepherd's contribution to Kent was apposite if understated: 'Shepherd's all-round ability proved extremely valuable. He had a rewarding season with bat and ball.'[118]

Highlights of Shepherd's 'rewarding' 1976 season included a fifty in each innings and five wickets in the match in an early-season fixture against Middlesex at Lord's. In Kent's first innings he hit '... a flurry of strokes, the

117 Peter Marson in *The Times*, 6 August 1975.
118 Dudley Moore in *Wisden*, 1977.

last of which [was] a beautifully timed straight drive, to the seats in front of the pavilion'[119] and in the second innings he hit 52, of which no fewer that 50 runs were in boundaries (11 fours and a six). Later in May Shep hit another boundary-filled innings of 73 against Hampshire at Southampton, but in June against Essex at Tunbridge Wells he had to retire from the match early on the first morning with severe back problems which were to keep him out of cricket for ten days. Soon after his return Shepherd was in good allround form in a high scoring draw with Nottinghamshire at Trent Bridge (58* and four for 89) and he showed that his bowling was back at its best with three for 60 and five for 69 against Hampshire at Maidstone. In July and August Shepherd enjoyed the rock-hard pitches and fast outfields with five fifties in the space of two weeks and later in August he caused Somerset to collapse at Taunton with another five-wicket haul. At the end of this personally productive season Shepherd had another fine allround match at Leicester where, coming to the wicket with Kent in trouble at 89 for four, he and Mike Denness rescued the innings with Shepherd making his highest score of the season, 87, with 14 fours and a six before being caught on the long leg boundary - he also took four for 62 in the Leicestershire first innings and was again Kent's top scorer in their second innings with 38.

Whilst John Shepherd was demonstrating once again his value to Kent, the direction of the county was meandering unwittingly into uncharted waters and missing the guiding hand of Les Ames on the tiller. Ames' successor as secretary, Eric Attenborough, had an unhappy three years in the job and left at the end of the 1976 season and his successor as cricket manager Colin Page was a less-than-sensitive man manager. The Chairman of the Cricket sub-Committee and his fellow committee members were also struggling to cope with the changing circumstances in the relationship between professional cricketers and amateur committee men - a problem that was to come further to a head in 1977. But at the end of the 1976 season the principal casualty in this leadership void was county captain Mike Denness. Denness, who had lost the England captaincy to Tony Greig in 1975, now relinquished the Kent captaincy in confused circumstances - a story which reflects badly on the bungling hierarchy of the club's management and the Machiavellian nature of some of the parties involved. The irony of all of these shenanigans was that by most standards Kent had enjoyed a very successful season. The Benson and Hedges Cup had been won in a stirring Lord's final against Worcestershire in July with John Shepherd playing his part, especially by breaking Kent's opponents' patient opening partnership and helping reduce them to 90 for four, a position from which they never recovered. There was also an extraordinary win in the Sunday League when five counties had been in the running before the final day. Kent scored 278 runs in their innings (7 runs per over which crucially boosted their season's run-rate) against Gloucestershire and then dismissed their opponents for a paltry 155 for a comfortable win

119 Peter Marson in *The Times*, 30 April 1976.

– they 'batted like heroes and fielded like demons' and 'played like men inspired'.[120] Of the five counties who finished on 40 points, all with ten wins, Kent finished top and won on more away wins and a better run-rate. The star of the show at Maidstone on that final day had been Asif Iqbal who scored an imperious 108 and John Shepherd got the crucial breakthrough again by breaking Gloucestershire's opening partnership of 60 and then dismissing the dangerous Zaheer Abbas for two.

Two trophies in 1976, and four others earlier under his captaincy, were not enough to save the Kent captaincy job for Mike Denness and it was announced in October that Asif Iqbal would succeed him as captain for the 1977 season. Denness moved on to Essex where he enjoyed four successful seasons before his retirement in 1980.

On the last of John Shepherd's Southern African tours, with the International Wanderers in March/April 1976, he had become very friendly with his fellow tourists, the Australian captain Ian Chappell and his compatriot Alan Hurst. A consequence of these friendships was that it was suggested that Shep, instead of returning to Rhodesia for the 1976/1977 season as he had planned to do, came and played top-class grade cricket in Australia. This turned into an offer from the Melbourne side Footscray. Shepherd, his wife Terry and their baby daughter Caroline travelled out to Australia for the first time at the end of the 1976 English season. It was to be the ideal winter employment. Footscray found the Shepherd family a flat in the Geelong Road and he was well paid as the club's full-time professional and coach. Players at the club included Alan Hurst and Ray Bright, and Shepherd also coached the fifteen-year-old Dean Jones and the even younger Tony Dodemaide.

The playing commitment was in two-day grade games at the weekend – it was intense cricket of a very high standard and the main nursery of Australian professional cricket. As the only professional, Shepherd believed that he had to be on top of his game in every match and his contribution was indeed exceptional. In one match against Melbourne he hit 156 in 162 balls, including 6 sixes and 11 fours, and across the season as a whole he scored 458 runs in 12 innings at 38.16 and took 32 wickets at 14.34 to help Footscray to the State finals. This led to him being given, by a record margin, the coveted Jack Ryder Medal, awarded to the Victorian cricketer of the season and voted for by the District umpires. He also won the *Age/Puma* and *Sunday Press/CP Air* cricket awards that season. The Shepherd family found their Aussie hosts most hospitable – including Ian Chappell with whom they spent Christmas in Adelaide.

1977

On his return to England after his successful winter in Australia John Shepherd was to find that there was uncertainty in the air when he

120 Brian Chapman, *The Guardian*, 6 September 1976.

reported for duty at Canterbury in April. The triumph of two one-day trophies the previous year was tempered by the fall in the County Championship to fourteenth - the lowest position for twenty years. And with Denness and Luckhurst gone from the playing staff, and Asif something of an unknown quantity as captain, it was clearly to be a time of change. During his months in Australia Shepherd had heard rumours that something sensational was brewing in the world of cricket but he was taken by surprise when, on 10 May, the news broke of Kerry Packer's signing of eighteen Australians and seventeen other international players for his 'Super Test' series in Australia in 1977/78. The internationals from outside Australia included his county colleagues Underwood, Knott and his new captain, Asif Iqbal. They were soon to be joined by Bob Woolmer and Bernard Julien, so Kent was to provide five players for Mr Packer's 'circus'. It could have been six - Shepherd himself was committed to Footscray and although informal approaches were made to him from 'World Series Cricket' (as Packer's enterprise was known) he elected to stay loyal to the Victoria grade side for another season rather than indicate to WSC that he was interested.

John Shepherd had finished the 1976 season with a haul of nine wickets in his last two Championship matches and he soon showed that his form had not slipped as the 1977 season got under way. He suffered briefly from a shoulder injury but had shrugged this off by mid-May when in Bristol he took nine wickets in a match to help Kent beat Gloucestershire by an innings. Shortly after this there were nine wickets again as Kent trounced Middlesex at Dartford. But these feats were to be topped by an extraordinary performance in a rain-affected match against Lancashire during Tunbridge Wells week. Under leaden skies he took eight for 83 in 37 overs - one of three occasions in his career that he took eight wickets in an innings. By 17 June Shep had taken 36 wickets for Kent in all competitions and many more were to come. A rare 'Man of the Match' award came later in June but this time it was Shepherd's batting that was rewarded as he almost single-handedly helped Kent post a respectable score of 226 in the first round of the Gillette Cup against Middlesex. Coming in with the county in trouble at 47 for five, he played one of the best innings of his career scoring 101, reaching his century, his only one in one-day cricket, in the last of the 60 overs. Despite Shepherd's heroics Kent was to lose this match, but they fared better in the Benson and Hedges competition reaching the final at Lord's in July where they were beaten by a Gloucestershire side responding well to Mike Procter's inspired leadership. Kent chased 238 for victory but only Woolmer (64) and Shepherd (55) held up 'Proctershire's' march to victory. There was frustration as well in the Sunday League where the title won so dramatically in 1976 was lost and Kent slipped to sixth in the table. But these one-day disappointments paled into insignificance as the county made a spirited attack on the County Championship. It was in this competition that John Shepherd's bowling came dramatically to the fore - he took 87 wickets at a remarkably economical average of 19.93 and only Mike Procter and Ian Botham took more wickets in first-class cricket in England in 1977 than Shepherd.

As Kent's push for the Championship intensified, Shep played a key part in wins against Essex (one wicket) and Nottinghamshire (eight wickets). There was also a fine allround performance in a crucial win over Yorkshire in July when Shep and Alan Ealham turned Kent's first innings round with a partnership of 109 for the seventh wicket (Shepherd 63) and Shep also took five wickets in the match. As Kent entered the final Championship match of the season against Warwickshire at Edgbaston in early September they were joint second in the table with Middlesex and five points behind Gloucestershire. Gloucestershire faltered in their final match losing to Hampshire, but with Middlesex beating Lancashire and gaining 16 points the news filtered down to Kent at teatime that on the final afternoon of the season they needed to win at Edgbaston to secure 16 points themselves and tie the championship with Middlesex. Kent had been put in a potentially winning position - despite a disastrous first innings of only 118 - by the bowling of Woolmer (three for 32) and, inevitably, Shepherd who had another five-wicket haul, for 63, in Warwickshire's 181. Then when Kent batted a second time they faltered again to 148 for five before the Ealham/Shepherd partnership fired once more in a stand of 74 and, with Shepherd top-scoring with 77, Kent reached 316 leaving Warwickshire 253 for victory . It looked all over when Warwickshire collapsed to 29 for five but in the end Kent won by only 27 runs as their opponents recovered to 226 all out. A fine Kent win and their second post-war Championship was thus added to their success in 1970, albeit that this time the trophy was shared. And John Shepherd's part in this achievement was rightly acknowledged by all at the county - as the quote from *Wisden* at the head of this chapter records. In all cricket for Kent in 1977 Shep took 100 wickets, scored 766 runs and held 21 catches.

The tensions in English cricket that Packer-clouded summer were well captured by John Woodcock in *The Times* when reporting on Kent's final match. Kent were being frustrated by a last-wicket partnership in their chase for victory and one of the participants in that partnership was the England stalwart David Brown. Woodcock wrote that 'No one in English cricket ... would have been keener to deny Kent, riddled as they are with Packer recruits, than Brown the leader of the anti-Packer lobby.'[121] The Kent committees were certainly embarrassed by the fact that the county had so many Packer signatories in their dressing room and then soon took steps to get rid of one of them - Bernard Julien was not offered terms for 1978 and intense discussions were also taking place about the future of the captain, Asif Iqbal. But for John Shepherd there was happier news. The Kent General Committee met in November 1977 and agreed that their long-serving stalwart could have a benefit in 1979[122] and Shep was soon to receive a letter from Jim Swanton confirming that this was the case.

121 John Woodcock, *The Times*, 10 September 1977.
122 Minutes of Kent C.C.C. General Committee, 10 November 1977.

The Packer affair was to rumble on for the rest of 1977 but the Australian's battle with the cricket establishment was to work out entirely in his favour with the High Court ruling on 25 November that the ICC and the TCCB could not preclude Packer players from returning to county cricket. Indeed, Underwood, Woolmer and Asif Iqbal were all to play a full season for Kent in 1978 although Alan Knott took a year off, before returning to the county in 1979.

Shepherd returned to skipper Footscray in Australia for the 1977/78 season and was successful again with fine allround performances for the Melbourne grade club, taking 48 wickets and scoring 450 runs. This included one match against St Kilda in which Shep took seven for 27 in the opponents' first innings and eight for 10 in the second. As in the previous year he polled 36 votes in the 1977/78 Ryder Medal, but this time he finished equal third behind Keith Stackpole (38) and Mick Taylor (37).

1978

On the morning of 28 March 1978 Kent's Cricket sub-Committee met to discuss, among other things, the captaincy of the county for the 1978 season. As we have seen, the fact that this was on the table at all after Asif Iqbal's successes in 1977 was entirely due to Asif's participation in the Packer 'World Series Cricket' matches the previous winter. The sub-Committee recommended that Asif be reappointed but recorded that as there was a 'probability that [this recommendation] would be rejected by the General Committee ... [they] should consider an alternative nomination'. They then 'discussed the most suitable candidates, in particular Messrs A.Ealham, J.Shepherd, G. Johnson and M.C.Cowdrey were mentioned. It was decided by five votes to two that in the event of Asif Iqbal's appointment not being confirmed to recommend Alan Ealham for the captaincy.'[123] The sub-committee was right that the General Committee would reject Asif and indeed they went further by terminating Asif's contract, along with the other Packer players, with effect from the end of the 1978 season.[124] 'A number of alternatives were then discussed, after which the name of Mr Alan Ealham was put to the Committee and he was elected captain for the 1978 season.'[125]

The Kent committees' wrestling with their consciences so close to the beginning of the 1978 season need not deter us now other than to reflect on the almost surreal nature of the debate – at least when viewed from the perspective of thirty years on! That Colin Cowdrey, by then aged 46, should actually have been discussed by the sub-committee seems bizarre. (Perhaps Colin's son Christopher, who had made his debut for the county

123 Minutes of Kent C.C.C. Cricket sub-Committee, 28 March 1978.

124 This decision was rescinded in July 1978 and all the Packer players were retained for 1979 and beyond. This led Brian Johnston to resign his Kent membership believing, as he said in *The Cricketer* magazine in October 1978, that Kent were wrong to put the county first ahead of the interests of England.

125 Minutes of Kent C.C.C. General Committee, 28 March 1978.

in 1977, was seen not to be quite ready at the age of 20.) How close John Shepherd came to being chosen, especially in the light of his fine year in 1977 and his experience,[126] we cannot know – although Derek Underwood's view that '... at that time I don't think that [Kent] would have wanted a West Indian captain'[127] has the ring of truth about it.

Alan Ealham had the good fortune in his first year as captain to be able to turn out a full side, week after week, untroubled by Test match demands. His first match as captain of Kent was a Benson and Hedges group match at Canterbury against Yorkshire on 22 April 1978 and, notwithstanding the intrigues of the winter, the dressing room had a familiar look to it. Asif, Woolmer and Underwood were back from Packer duties, John Shepherd was back from another successful sojourn with Footscray in Melbourne and the promising younger players Tavaré (23), Cowdrey (20), Hills (27), Downton (20) and Jarvis (24) completed the line-up along with vice-captain Graham Johnson. Would all the problems the county had faced over the winter disrupt the players? Would the accidental captain Alan Ealham be up to the job? Would the Packer 'stars', who would be available for the whole season for the first time for years, add to the county's strength significantly? Would Knotty be missed? And wouldn't Shep, now aged 34, at last begin to creak a bit at the joints? Well in fact John Shepherd did suffer from a nagging ankle/heel injury for some of the season but, as *Wisden* 1979 recorded, he was still to enjoy a fine season with bat and ball'[128] in 1978 and, as we shall see, this was to be marked by the cricketers' bible in a very special way at the beginning of Shep's benefit year.

The bare statistics of John Shepherd's 1978 season suggest a slightly lessened workload with the ball (758 overs in all competitions and 78 wickets) and something of an *annus mirabilis* with the bat (1,155 runs and an average of 32 and two first-class centuries). But the figures hide the fact that, with Underwood available for every match, the workload on the other bowlers could be somewhat reduced – only somewhat in Shepherd's case as he was still the workhorse of the side and second only to Underwood in the number of first-class overs bowled. Under Alan Ealham's astute captaincy Shep was used cleverly in the one-day matches which led not only to his being the leading wicket-taker but to an astonishingly economical average of 13.91. Bowling highlights included a seven-wicket haul in May against Somerset in Taunton, including the great Viv Richards clean bowled first ball, and eight wickets against Middlesex in the space of two days in early June (four for 22 on the Saturday in the County Championship and four for 17 on the Sunday in that league). The value of Shepherd's bowling in one-day competitions in 1978 was exemplified by successive matches in July; in the Gillette Cup on the 19th he took four for 38 against Northamptonshire and three days later on the 22nd he took four

126 The *World of Cricket* annual of 1978, edited by Trevor Bailey, said of Shepherd's 1977 performances, '... the older he grows the more shrewd he becomes'.

127 Interview with the author, 24 September 2008.

128 *Wisden Cricketers' Almanack*, 1979.

for 25 in the Benson and Hedges Cup final at Lord's against Derbyshire – both matches which Kent won.

For some seasons successive Kent captains had been using John Shepherd as a flexible resource with the bat. When the county boasted as many as seven players in the side who had scored centuries in Test cricket,[129] as they did at times in the mid-1970s, then Shep would bat well down the order, but when Test calls reduced the batting strength he would be promoted. In 1978 the Kent team was in transition which meant that both the new captain and John Shepherd had to accept a more prominent batting role. Both responded admirably, with Ealham usually batting at No.5 in the Championship averaging over 30 and Shepherd, promoted to six, scoring 785 runs at an impressive 35.68. Batting highlights included a hard-hit 58 against Middlesex at Lord's which Colin Cowdrey remembered as including Shep despatching ' ... a good length ball from John Emburey onto the top tier of the pavilion, the largest hit I have ever seen.'[130] There was also a fine century against Surrey at Tunbridge Wells in June. Coming to the crease with Kent on 131 for four, he put on 112 with Ealham and completed his hundred (a six and 14 fours) in less than three hours just before Ealham declared at 311 for six – Kent won the match by an innings. In July Kent had to chase a total of 223 in 225 minutes for victory in a key Championship match against Glamorgan at Maidstone. The loss of three wickets for only 36 runs slowed the chase but this brought Shepherd to the crease and together with Chris Tavaré he saw Kent home with 12 overs to spare, scoring 65* with 3 sixes and 9 fours. This was Kent's ninth Championship win in thirteen matches and it took them 26 points clear at the top of the table. Hopes were high for retention of the Championship title and that Kent would be sole winners this time. And so it proved – an unbeaten run took the county to the title by the third week in August and they eventually finished a comfortable 19 points clear of Essex to win their sixth and to date[131] last County Championship. During the run-in John Shepherd had scored another century, his seventh in first-class cricket, 100* against Worcestershire at New Road to help set up another Kent win.

The Championship triumph was just what the Doctor would have ordered and his namesake Colonel Grace, the Kent President elect, had another trophy to celebrate as well when they moved fairly effortlessly to another Benson and Hedges final – this time against Derbyshire. It was a one-sided match once John Shepherd, swinging the ball prodigiously, had helped dismiss Derbyshire for 147 – he took four for 25 in 11 tight overs and then with Kent slightly worrying their supporters at 117 for four, he and Ealham quietly steered them to victory with 13 overs to spare and well before six o'clock. John Woodcock enthused in *The Times* about Kent: 'Twice winners of the Gillette Cup, three times of the Sunday League and now three times

129 Denness, Luckhurst, Cowdrey, Woolmer, Julien, Asif Iqbal and Knott.
130 Colin Cowdrey, 'A true man of Kent' in *John Shepherd Benefit Souvenir*, 1979.
131 Up to the end of the 2008 season during which Kent was relegated to the lower division of the two-tier Championship for the first time.

of the Benson and Hedges, their one-day record is second to none.'[132] In the context of this record the county's slip to eleventh in the Sunday League in 1978 was perhaps the only disappointment in a magnificent season. It was to be seventeen years before Kent was to win another trophy - the Sunday League in 1995 - but that's another story.

The John Shepherd cricket story happily did not finish at the end of the 1978 season, as we shall see, but in many ways that season was the apotheosis of his career. In June he was asked to captain the county for the first time, in a Championship match against Middlesex at Lord's. He led Kent to a fine win, taking four wickets in the home team's first innings and scoring a hard-hitting 58, including a six which hit the rail of the top balcony of the pavilion. Chasing 96 to win in their second innings, Kent got home comfortably in the end with Shepherd and Cowdrey junior scoring the winning runs for a six-wicket victory. As the two batsmen entered the Lord's pavilion Shepherd was surprised that John Pocock, who was Chairman of Kent's Cricket sub-Committee, ignored him. Shep's colleague, the young Charles Rowe, noticed this apparent slight. 'Perhaps Pocock didn't support you as captain Shep?' he said - and in the light of the committee's deliberations in March perhaps Rowe was right.

When the Kent Annual for 1979 was published, John Shepherd, the year's beneficiary, was pictured on the front cover proudly clutching the 'Kent Cricketer of the Year' trophy. But a greater honour was to be granted shortly for, when *Wisden* published their 1979 almanack, Shep had been chosen as one of their five 'Cricketers of the Year'.[133] The brief biography in *Wisden* captures well Shep's career and few would challenge their statement that 'Shepherd has reigned comfortably as one of the most successful all-rounders in the world ... .' But in 1979 and beyond even tougher challenges, both cricketing and personal, lay ahead.

---

132 John Woodcock, *The Times*, 24 July 1978.
133 The other four were David Gower, John Lever, Chris Old and Clive Radley.

Chapter Seven

Kent: The Final Years

He has, in my opinion, given the best value of any overseas player to play in English County cricket. The service he has given Kent on the field is tremendous. The service he has given off the field, with his modesty, good manners and sense of humour, may be worth even more. When he retires it will be terribly hard to replace him - perhaps impossible - for he has been the heart of this side for 12 years - years in which we have accomplished so much.

Colin Page, Kent Cricket Manager, February 1980[134]

1979

By the beginning of the 1979 season John Shepherd, newly acclaimed as one of *Wisden*'s five 'Cricketers of the Year', and the Kent beneficiary for the year, had played 301 first-class matches, scoring 9,746 runs (at 26.19 including seven centuries) and taking 847 wickets (at 26.21 including five wickets in an innings 45 times). Of all the players in county cricket in 1979 only fourteen had taken more wickets in their careers to date than Shep and only five of these could be seen to be genuine allrounders (Tony Greig, Ray Illingworth, Intikhab Alam, Fred Titmus and Mike Procter - distinguished company). In addition, of course, Shepherd had played twelve seasons of top-flight one-day cricket for Kent scoring over 3,000 runs and taking over 250 wickets. If ever anyone had earned that benefit it was Shepherd.

Preparation for the benefit began over the 1978/79 winter, and this meant that a third season at Footscray was not possible. All of Shep's efforts and those of the team of helpers he recruited were directed towards the task of having a successful benefit. 'Semi-feudal' [135] the system might have been but, as a source of funds to assure a loyal county cricketer some financial security once his cricket days were over, it was essential - especially as the money raised was not liable to income or other taxes. The main source of funds was the so-called 'pontoon jars' which were placed on the bars at pubs and clubs across the county - with the agreement of their landlords. They were basically lucky-dip draws with a top prize of £10 and with

134 Interview given to Jack Beaumont of the London Press Service.
135 Bob Willis, with Patrick Murphy, *Cricket Revolution*, Book Club Associates, 1981.

tickets being sold at 50p. Norman Graham had set the standard in 1977 – his success being attributable both to his popularity and to the fact that his face was very familiar in pubs across the county. Big Norm's benefit was officially around £58,000 but in reality probably a lot more. Shep was equally popular, although his lifestyle was rather less pub-focused so he had to work a bit harder to rival Graham's rewards. And work hard he did, with personal appearances at all of his official events, such as golf days and cricket matches, as well as frequent trips to the pubs to advance the pontoon jar takings – on one day in the Deal and Dover area he and his local benefit organiser Fred Wilson visited no fewer than 21 pubs in the one evening alone!

John Shepherd's 52-page benefit brochure included tributes from a distinguished list of contributors, including Les Ames, Colin Cowdrey, Jim Swanton, John Arlott, Ian Botham, Ali Bacher, Barry Richards, Alan Ealham and Bob Woolmer. Even allowing for the laudatory nature of the genre, the pieces are genuinely warm and complimentary. Colin Page perhaps summed up the feelings of all when he wrote that he regarded John Shepherd as the ' ... overseas cricketer [who] has contributed most to his adopted English county.'[136] For his benefit match Shepherd chose a Sunday League game against Worcestershire at Canterbury in August and there was a crowd of 9,000 and the collection raised £1,074 – a county record. Beneficiaries customarily get a courtesy 'one off the mark' in their benefit matches but Shep was out for a duck, caught at the wicket off the bowling of his fellow Southern African pioneer Younis Ahmed – and Kent narrowly lost the match.

After his sparkling year in 1978 when his allround performance for Kent fully justified Colin Page's claim, John Shepherd's cricketing year 1979 was something of a disappointment. His workload was slightly reduced; he played in 16 of Kent's 24 first-class matches and also missed a few of the one-day games and his number of overs bowled in the Championship, 418.3, was the lowest of any of his full seasons in the game. The runs also dried up somewhat in the Championship – 370 at 19.47, although he finished second in the county's one-day averages, scoring 395 runs at 28.21. It was common for players to struggle in their benefit years – something that was broadly accepted by the county management. John Shepherd's normal commitment and loyalty was tested as there were benefit events to plan and to manage – this inevitably played on his mind even, unwittingly, on the field of play. In the Kent eleven Chris Tavaré and Graham Dilley were firmly establishing their places, and Bob Woolmer was the leading batsman and there was a good run in the Sunday League which, had the county beaten Middlesex in front of a full house at Canterbury on the final day, would have seen them take the trophy. It was not to be and Middlesex won comfortably to relegate Kent to runners-up. The 1980 Kent

136 Colin Page, in *John Shepherd Benefit Souvenir*, 1979. Dudley Moore in *Wisden*'s 'Cricketer of the Year' tribute reported that Shep did not think of himself 'as an overseas player, just a member of the Kent team.'

Annual Report description of Shepherd's 1979 season as 'disappointing' was perhaps fair, although their charge that he was 'plagued by injury and ill-health' was overstated. There were some highlights - a 'violent' 86 with 3 sixes and 8 fours in the Championship versus Middlesex at Lord's in May and six wickets in the match in the return at Tunbridge Wells in June when Shepherd bowled 54 overs across the two innings - no lack of effort there!

There are suggestions that the Kent committees were beginning to think of a future without John Shepherd. For example, the minutes of the Cricket sub-Committee meeting on 20 November 1979 record that 'The Cricket Manager [Colin Page] said that during a recent tour of Antigua he had seen a young West Indian, S.Baptiste aged 18,[137] who he considered might be a replacement for John Shepherd as an allrounder'. Not too much should be read into this although, as we shall see, Shepherd's position was to become more precarious in 1980 and 1981.

John Shepherd's benefit of around £60,000[138] was a record for Kent and for the first time in his life he began to feel financially secure. Returning to Barbados for the winter, he decided that he would use half of the money to buy a house there, partly as a long-term investment and partly to give himself and his family the option of returning to the island of his birth at some time in the future.

1980

With the benefit year successfully behind him, John Shepherd returned to Kent at the beginning of the 1980 season to commence his sixteenth year as an employee of the county. He was slightly late arriving back from Barbados and this led to his being fined £178 by Kent - a curiously precise sum. Shep resented the suggestion that he had been casual in not getting back to Kent on time: 'I was not gallivanting about - I trained out there but was involved in buying property', he said![139] At the age of 36 he was, as the previous year had suggested, creaking a little at the seams but his underlying physical strength remained good and his Kent experience was unequalled. Apart from the unique Derek Underwood, Shepherd had taken more first-class wickets by far than any other player on the staff and his runs total was bettered only by Knott, Asif and (just) by the fast-improving Bob Woolmer. Although he had been overlooked for the captaincy, Shepherd's match experience and sound cricket brain was also being tapped frequently by his friend Alan Ealham, whose own position as captain after two seasons might be threatened if Kent did not return to trophy-winning form in 1980.

It was to be a very wet year. A number of Kent players were on international duty on and off throughout the summer (Woolmer, Tavare, Knott, Dilley

137 Eldine Baptiste was to play for the county from 1981 to 1987.
138 Equivalent to around £230,000 in 2009 money.
139 Reported in *The Cricketer* magazine, July 1980.

and Underwood) and their replacements failed to make much of an impact – but even the mostly ever-present players, including John Shepherd, had moderate seasons and the team as a whole struggled to be competitive. The bowling was generally weak and, as *Wisden* records, Shepherd 'plagued by niggling injuries, battled away to alleviate the obvious deficiencies in attack.'[140] Battle he certainly did – his 473.1 overs in first-class matches was a workload second only to that of Underwood, and he was also the mainstay of the attack and the leading wicket-taker in the one-day competitions. But the county drifted from one poor result to another. They were knocked out by Yorkshire in the first round of the Gillette Cup; lost three of the four B&H group games and did not progress further; and won only six of their sixteen Sunday League matches to slip to eleventh in the table.

In the Championship Kent won only twice and plummeted to sixteenth in the table. In July there was an innings defeat to Nottinghamshire at Trent Bridge where, in their first innings, Kent was bowled out for just 67 – a match that John Shepherd missed. For Shepherd there were a few moments of bright light in the general gloom – a stunning 100 in 118 balls at Maidstone (2 sixes and 9 fours) against Surrey rescued Kent from a parlous 88 for six, although the match was eventually abandoned as a draw. Alan Ross described Shepherd as being ' ... portly and pugnacious, plundering each bowler in turn. He hooked Jackman to the boundary in the first over ... he went happily on his way sweeping and driving to his first hundred in two years."[141] Shep's 'portly' appearance was probably more due to his being wrapped up against the elements than to any incipient middle-aged spread! And how he enjoyed dispatching his old 'Rhodesian' adversary Robin Jackman to the boundary in such cavalier style! In his next innings Shep continued this good form with another hard-hitting innings against Somerset – 60 with 2 sixes and 7 fours helped Kent to some respectability after early struggles. With the ball there was hard work very often with little reward. An exception was against Yorkshire at Sheffield in June when on a lively pitch he took five for 40 in 19.2 overs – but there were few other highlights, just hard graft. And for Alan Ealham's captaincy it was to be the end – Asif Iqbal, forgiven for his Packer 'misdemeanours' and the recent controversy when appearing for Pakistan against India overlooked, would be back in charge for 1981 – which was also his benefit season. This sacking of Ealham after only three years, the first of which at least had been spectacularly successful, was not universally welcomed and the appointment of Asif was seen by many commentators as a further error of judgment by the Kent committees. Robin Marlar, for example, said that 'There are times when the Kent committee presents itself ... poorly. They did so at the time of the Packer crisis and they have done so again by choosing Asif Iqbal for a second term ... an appointment which is bad both for English cricket and for cricketers in England.'[142]

140 Dudley Moore in *Wisden* 1981.
141 Alan Ross, *The Times*, 12 July 1980.
142 Robin Marlar, *The Cricketer*, January 1981.

1981

On 9 June 1980 Kent's Cricket sub-Committee had met and discussed the season so far, which at that early point was not looking good. A discussion about the playing staff for 1981 ensued and the committee's minutes record that they were

> disappointed at the form of John Shepherd and Asif Iqbal and [Colin Page] stated that it was the intention to rest these two players and to give some of the younger players the opportunity of experiencing playing in the first eleven. Serious discussion was also given to the future of these two players ... and it was agreed that the Chairman of the sub-Committee (Arthur Phebey) and Colin Page should discuss the question with the players concerned.

Whether any such discussions ever took place is not recorded and Shepherd today cannot recall that they did. But although Shep continued to be selected for the remainder of the season Asif was, as *Wisden* records ' ... side-lined ... Thus the best side was not always selected and a certain amount of confusion and frustration was caused.'[143] Asif weathered this storm so well that he actually recovered the Kent captaincy. But as far as Shepherd was concerned, and largely unknown to him, more sinister clouds were gathering. In the following sub-committee meeting in July it was recorded that 'The Chairman also agreed to inform John Shepherd that his services would be required in 1981', but there was no ringing endorsement of Shepherd forthcoming and no contract promises beyond the 1981 season. It was clear that the overriding emphasis of Kent's strategy at the time was to encourage younger players and that it was quite possible that a ruthless approach to the continued employment of the long-serving Shepherd was in the minds of the committees.

At the start of the 1981 season John Shepherd was unaware that his position was under any serious threat. On the contrary, his expectation was that in the years to come, as his first-team place began less certain, he would be asked to continue in a supportive and coaching role. It was not an unreasonable assumption. There was no more popular player on the Kent staff than Shep and none with his depth of experience. Combine this with a proven work ethic and an unconditional loyalty to the county that had employed him through most of his adult life and few at Kent would question that Shepherd had the potential to continue to make a contribution once his playing days were over. But, as far as Shepherd was concerned, that was to be some years away – he was as ready to play hard for Kent in 1981 as he always had been. Shepherd was not unaware that there had been some 'mutterings' about his position – committee rooms and dressing rooms are always gossipy and leaky places. A conversation with Brian Luckhurst had not been reassuring. Luckhurst was the Second Eleven captain and also the assistant to the Cricket Manager Colin Page. On

143 Dudley Moore, *Wisden*, 1981.

the eve of the 1981 season Page was taken ill and Luckhurst was appointed acting manager – he was confirmed as full-time Cricket Manager later in the year. Luckhurst had said to Shepherd that his recent (1979 and 1980) record was not really good enough and that Shep needed to ' ... show me some good results so they could keep him on'.

The removal of Ealham and the holding-operation appointment of Asif Iqbal at the age of 38 suggested that the Kent committees did not have confidence that a younger captain such as Tavaré or Chris Cowdrey was yet ready to assume the captaincy mantle. The shaky confidence of the committee men was matched in the dressing room where after two unsuccessful years, and with the after effects of Packer still rumbling, confidence was also low. By mid-June none of the six Championship matches played had been won and only one of the four Sunday League games. Kent was also out of the NatWest trophy, although qualification for the knock-out stages of the B&H had been achieved. John Shepherd was also struggling, uncertain of his future and conscious of the scuttlebutt about the need for Kent to choose younger players – especially the promising twenty-year-old allrounder Richard Ellison.

The first match of Tunbridge Wells week showed that the county's predilection for using Shep as a 'workhorse' had not changed and he was required to bowl 46 overs in the Leicestershire innings as David Gower helped himself to a sparkling century in the town of his birth. Shep took three wickets for 132 in a match reduced to one innings each and was also involved in a match-saving partnership, scoring 56*, when Kent batted. Later in the week Shep's workload was scarcely reduced with 25 overs in Sussex's first innings in a match in which Kent achieved one of their few Championship wins in the season. In early July he bowled 99.3 overs in the two Maidstone week matches and this was followed by a further 82 overs in away matches at Lord's and Leicester. In the Leicestershire match Shepherd and Jarvis bowled Kent to a fine victory with Shepherd reminding the Kent selectors and committee men that he could still take wickets with four for 42. On 23 July 1981, two days after Shep had helped Kent to win the Leicester match, the Cricket sub-Committee, under Arthur Phebey's chairmanship, was meeting with a full agenda including an item on 'Playing Staff for 1982'. Also at the meeting was Shep's colleague Bob Woolmer who was the players' representative on the committee – a fairly recent innovation – and Brian Luckhurst who, as we have seen, had been appointed acting Cricket Manager earlier in the season. The sub-Committee's minutes record the outcome of their deliberations on the playing staff issue:

> After a lengthy discussion it was agreed not to offer fresh contracts to the following players: N.J.Kemp, C.J.C.Rowe and J.N.Shepherd. The Committee were very appreciative of the service which all three players had given to the Club and especially wished to record the great contribution which John Shepherd had made to the Club's success in the 1970s.

The day after this meeting Bob Woolmer travelled to Derby where he was to join the Kent side for the Championship match against Derbyshire which began on Saturday 25 July. Waiting for him in the hotel was John Shepherd, who knew that the subject of player appointments had been discussed the day before. As Woolmer saw Shep he went bright red in the face and, although he could not disclose the discussions in the committee, for Shepherd his friend's face said it all. He had been sacked. Later in the month Brian Luckhurst explained Kent's reasoning to *The Guardian*: 'He [Shepherd] has given wonderful service over the years and must be one of the best value for money overseas players ever. We felt, however, that the time has come to look to the future and the young players coming up.'[144]

John Shepherd played only three more games for Kent after that momentous weekend in Derby. Sitting out one of Kent's end-of-season matches at Canterbury he sat next to Brian Luckhurst and said to Kent's Cricket Manager that he would be happy to make himself available on a match-by-match basis in 1982 – partly because with 953 wickets under his belt he wanted to pick up the 47 more he needed to achieve the rare feat of a thousand wickets in the first-class game.[145] Luckhurst replied that Shep must understand that Kent '... was not running a charity'. To say that John Shepherd, the loyalist of Kent servants, was incensed by this tactless remark from someone who had been a playing colleague of his for more than ten years would be an understatement. That Luckhurst came very close to getting a large clenched black fist in his face he probably never knew!

John Shepherd was distressed and disillusioned. He really found it impossible to believe that at the age of 37, after seventeen years with the County and, he believed, with at least two more seasons in him, his services had been so summarily dismissed. In particular he was aggrieved that the decision not to re-engage him had been handled with such crass insensitivity. The world of cricket agreed. Alan Lee in *The Cricketer* summed up the feelings of many in the game:

> It was galling, therefore, for him to discover the hard way that he was no longer wanted by the county he joined in 1966. *[sic]* There are undoubtedly good reasons for Kent's decision, but the manner in which it was made and transmitted to the Barbadian whose cheeriness has been such a feature of domestic cricket, seemed to some to be a little callous.[146]

John Shepherd's final match for Kent was in the Sunday League at Canterbury against Worcestershire on Sunday 13 September 1981 – he was given a warm send-off by the crowd for whom he had always been a special

144 *The Guardian*, 30 July 1984.

145 Amongst county cricket regulars only Geoff Arnold, Jack Birkenshaw, Norman Gifford, Ken Higgs, Robin Hobbs, Intikhab Alam, Robin Jackman, John Lever, Pat Pocock, Mike Procter and Derek Underwood had reached this landmark at the end of 1981.

146 Alan Lee in *The Cricketer*, October 1981.

favourite. There were champagne corks popping in the dressing room which prompted Shep, with a smile as ever, to inquire if anyone could tell him why he was celebrating being sacked. And that was that!

A litterateur among the county's supporters would later find a relevant quotation in Shakespeare. It appears in *Henry VI Part II*, where Jack Cade says, 'Tell Kent from me, she hath lost her best man.'

And that was that.
John Shepherd leads out the Kent side in his 250th and last 'List A' limited-overs match for the county.
At Canterbury against Worcestershire on 13 September 1981.

Chapter Eight
Third Innings

None worked harder to try to overcome bowling shortcomings than the new-ball pair ... John Shepherd, in his 40th year, had a splendid season, doing the modern equivalent of "the double" by claiming 67 wickets and scoring 1,025 runs. He was always fit and ready to bowl, and he more than maintained the high standards he has set himself throughout a long career.

Geoff Wheeler, Wisden Cricketers' Almanack, 1984

It is a harsh reality of the life of a professional sportsman that, at an age where those in other professions are getting into stride in their careers, the sportsman's first-choice livelihood is coming to an end. John Shepherd's performances for Kent since his benefit year had not been as sparkling as in earlier years, but there are extenuating circumstances and whilst age played a part, the shambolic nature of Kent's management at the time was arguably the primary cause. The retirement of Les Ames, the poor health and authoritarian management style of Colin Page and, especially, the lack of man-management skills of Page's successor, Brian Luckhurst, all played a part. Derek Underwood puts it succinctly: 'To be absolutely honest I don't think that [Luckhurst] was management material.'[147] The captain, Asif Iqbal, was also rather distant from the fray and had not promoted Shepherd's cause very strongly and neither he nor Luckhurst, nor anyone in the committee hierarchy, had been at all hands-on with Shep as he went through a sticky patch on the field of play. Even the most experienced of professionals lose form and confidence from time to time and that is when coaches come into their own. Shep received no arm around the shoulder at a time when he needed one - instead he had a kick in the teeth.

When the news about John Shepherd's non-retention by Kent broke at the end of July and it became known that he was seeking to continue for a year or two as a player, there was speculation around the counties about which would sign him. Middlesex were the early favourites - Shep had a remarkable track record at Lord's but no firm offer was made. Derbyshire did make Shepherd a formal offer, as did Gloucestershire, and it was the latter that he eventually accepted. Tony Brown, Gloucestershire's Secretary and Cricket Manager, explained why they wanted Shep:

147 Interview with the author, 24 September 2008.

> We see Shepherd very much as the man to fill the hole left by Procter's departure. John has been a marvellous servant to the game and is still a very fine allrounder. He will give a lot of guidance to the younger players, and I imagine he will have the incentive of proving to a few people that he can still play a bit.[148]

Mike Procter had been a great success at Gloucestershire – to the extent that the county had been nicknamed 'Proctershire' by some fans. The Gillette Cup had been won in 1973 and the B&H in 1977 but the county had limited resources both financially and amongst the playing staff – especially with Procter's retirement. In hiring John Shepherd, initially with a contract for the 1982 and 1983 seasons, but with an option for 1984, they had clearly seen not just his cricketing skills but also, and perceptively, the probability that he would be able to use his knowledge and experience to help younger members of the playing staff to develop their talents. He was a potential coach in the making from the moment he joined the county.

For John Shepherd the offer from Gloucestershire was a big weight off his shoulders. Although his benefit year had significantly improved his financial position, the demands of a very young family meant that his wife was not able to work and although his final year's salary at Kent of £6,325 (plus bonuses) had not been munificent it was vital that he quickly found similarly remunerated employment. In fact he was offered an increase by Gloucestershire where he was paid £6,800 in his first year. The family moved to the Bristol area and in early May Shep played his first game for the county against Oxford University in The Parks. As had been the case in his first match for the Kent seconds in 1965 and in his first County Championship match in 1967, Shep scored a 50 on his debut – as well as taking three wickets in the University innings.

1982

In 1982, almost inevitably, John Shepherd bore the brunt of Gloucestershire's bowling attack – he was an ever-present in the side and his 742 overs in the County Championship and 161 overs in one-day games comfortably exceeded the workload of any other Gloucester player. In the absence, for much of the season, of a true strike bowler, Shepherd opened the county's bowling frequently and his 89 wickets in all competitions at an average of 31 suggested that Gloucestershire's investment was already paying off handsomely. Amongst the bowling highlights was a six-wicket haul on a cloudy day against Sussex at Hastings in May – *Wisden* said that Shep 'toiled magnificently to take six for 75 ... bowling unchanged on the slowish wicket until the final few overs.' There was also an 'inspired spell of seam bowling'[149] at Bradford in July which set up a good win against a hitherto undefeated Yorkshire. Shepherd generally batted down the order at seven in both the Championship and the one-day games – he scored 843

148 Quoted by Alan Lee in *The Cricketer*, December 1981.
149 *The Times*, 14 July 1982.

runs in all matches, his highest season's tally since 1978. In early August Gloucestershire played a NatWest Trophy quarter-final against Middlesex at Bristol. They dismissed their opponents for 215 with Shepherd taking two wickets and at 161 for four they were on track for a comfortable victory, but a late-order collapse and a couple of run-outs eventually saw Middlesex home by three runs. It was quiet in the dressing room after the match and the 'old pro' Shep was particularly despondent when the Chairman of the Gloucestershire Cricket Committee came in and brightly said: 'Bad luck lads - we gave them a game.' The usually mild Shepherd exploded at this rather condescending encouragement: 'We're not ****ing paid to give people games - we're paid to win!' he said.

A milestone reached.
John Shepherd with the scorecard showing his one-thousandth wicket in first-class cricket and the ball he used.
He dismissed Roland Butcher for 173 in the match Gloucestershire v Middlesex at Cheltenham on 12 August 1982.

There were few wins in Shepherd's first season at Gloucestershire and the county finished fifteenth in the Championship and fourteenth in the Sunday League. But on a personal level Shepherd was content that he had bowled his heart out to good effect and shown to his new colleagues that he was more than worth his place in the side. And he had shown to Kent, who had a dreadful season in Asif's last year as captain, what they were missing. Shep also captained Gloucestershire three times during the season when the captain David Graveney was absent.

1983

The double of 100 first-class wickets and 1,000 first-class runs, which John Shepherd had so narrowly missed back in 1968, had been redefined by *Wisden's Cricketers' Almanack* from the 1969 season onwards to reflect the reduction in the number of first-class matches played. From that year *Wisden* had recorded those cricketers in an English domestic season that had taken 50 wickets and scored 1,000 runs. It was a select list, comprising mostly the great allrounders such as Garry Sobers, Mushtaq Mohammad, Tony Greig, Mike Procter, Imran Khan, Clive Rice and Ian Botham. In 1983 John Shepherd was to join this distinguished list for, at the age of 39, he scored 1,025 runs and took 67 wickets in the season.[150] In addition he scored 196 runs and took 36 wickets in one-day matches. It was an astounding achievement which seemed to surprise even Gloucestershire's captain David Graveney, who eulogised:

> John Shepherd has also been in outstanding form with both bat and ball following a settling-in period last season, which was always going to be difficult for a player who had served Kent so loyally over many years. He has emerged this season as probably the most effective allrounder in the country despite his age, and regarding this delicate matter, I know that he takes much pride in the fact that many younger players have decided to call it a day! [151]

What had characterised John Shepherd's cricket in his glory years at Kent had been his ability to adapt his game to the circumstances of the match and the needs of the team. Barely a match passed without there being a significant contribution with bat or ball or in the field. This was to be the case in 1983, although generally in a losing cause, for Gloucestershire finished twelfth in the Championship, fourteenth in the Sunday League and bowed out in the quarter-final stages in the two knock-out tournaments. At Kent, Shep's contribution had been to a team glistening with stars – at Gloucester, only Zaheer Abbas, the grouchy Chris Broad, who was to leave the county at the end of the year, and Jack Russell in his first full season could be regarded like Shepherd as top-class players.

150 Shepherd's first-class run total was his second highest in an English season (1,157 in 1968 was the highest) and his average of 36.61 was also his second highest (38.91 in 1976 was the best). His total of 67 first-class wickets was his fifth highest.

151 David Graveney in his 'Captain's Column' in *The Cricketer*, August 1983.

In the third week in May John Shepherd had an allround match at Edgbaston against Warwickshire which was arguably his finest in the first-class game. On the first day he took seven for 50, one of his best returns in seventeen years of County Championship cricket. John Woodcock in *The Times* was clearly delighted by Shep's success ' ... the old fox bowled splendidly'. Later he wrote ' ... after lunch he trundled happily away until tea taking five wickets in the process. Six months short of his fortieth birthday he has worked hard at his fitness, which with that great torso of his he must have needed to do.'[152] The following day Shepherd surpassed even this performance when, coming to the wicket when Gloucestershire were 74 for four, he played the second highest innings of his life, 168, with 5 sixes and 22 fours, in a partnership of 268 with David Graveney to guide Gloucester to 382 for eight declared. John Woodcock, under the headline 'Shepherd ready to be led into the England fold', now called for Shepherd to be picked for the England side in the World Cup which was to be played in England in June.[153] And Matthew Engel in *The Guardian* suggested that Gloucestershire now be called 'Shepherdshire'![154]

As the World Cup was reaching its climax Shepherd had to settle for the rather more mundane world of county cricket which he did with a continued deluge of runs and flurry of wickets. There was a pugnacious 69 against Northants, 95* against Leicester where an overnight declaration denied Shep his century and then, in the following match at Bristol, a strong Kent team were the visitors. On the first day of the Championship match Shep was awarded his county cap during the lunch interval, which he celebrated by scoring a century after lunch and the following day, also against Kent, he had his best limited-overs figures of six for 52. To complete a productive few days against his old county Shepherd took four for 42 on the last day of the Championship match, including the wickets of Underwood and Knott. Remarkably the following day, at Bath, Shep took five for 80 on the first day of the Championship match against Somerset – fifteen wickets in three days in three different matches – and no burn-out in sight!

There were more riches in store in this true *annus mirabilis* before the end of the season including another astonishing allround performance in August in the Championship match against Glamorgan at Cheltenham. Shep scored 98*, running out of partners as he guided Gloucestershire to 376. Then he took two wickets and two catches to help skittle Glamorgan for 204 and, when their opponents followed on, he took seven for 64 to steer the County to an innings victory.

Over the season as a whole, in all matches John Shepherd had eight innings of 50 or more and took four or more wickets in an innings on seven

---

152 *The Times*, 26 and 27 May 1983.

153 Woodcock said that as it was more than ten years since Shepherd had played for the West Indies he was now eligible for England. Sadly the England selectors did not take the distinguished *Times* correspondent's advice.

154 'The timely Shepherd tends the flock', *The Guardian*, 27 May 1983.

occasions - small wonder that he was an ever-present in the Gloucestershire side that summer.

1984

John Shepherd celebrated his fortieth birthday on 9 November 1983 and looked forward after the extraordinary events of the year to another full season with Gloucestershire in 1984 which, realistically, he saw as being likely to be his last full year in first-class cricket. Could he leave the stage with the spectators still asking for more? In fact Shep was in many ways the man on the burning deck as Gloucestershire had a truly woeful season, finishing bottom in the County Championship, thirteenth in the Sunday League and failing to progress in either of the one-day competitions - including an embarrassing loss to the Combined Universities in the B&H. It was a weak side, ill-led by Graveney who nevertheless survived a vote of confidence at the end of the season. Even the emerging administrative and political talents of the young David Collier, in his second year as Secretary/Manager, could not help the struggling county. But for John Shepherd it was a hard working and personally successful season; he topped the county's first-class bowling averages and his tally of 72 wickets was by far the highest amongst all the bowlers. He also scored 846 first-class runs cementing, in his last full season, his record of nearly always being one of the leading allrounders in English domestic cricket. In what was indeed to be his final full year in premier-level cricket Shepherd took 97 wickets in all competitions and scored 1,084 runs - not bad for a man in his forty-first year! Personal highlights included a return to Canterbury in June where he took three wickets for 2 runs in twelve balls in Kent's first innings (four for 39 in all) and then five for 30 (including Woolmer, Tavare and Knott) as the home side was skittled out for 70 in their second innings to set up a rare Gloucestershire win. On nine occasions in the season Shepherd took four or more wickets in an

Another hard-working season. Shepherd took 72 first-class wickets in 1984.

innings and he also delivered seven scores of fifty or more. Two of the half-centuries were in the same match versus his favourite opponents Middlesex at Uxbridge where he top-scored in both innings and almost single-handedly set up an improbable win.

On 9 July 1984 John Shepherd was playing in a Sunday League match against Yorkshire at Scarborough along with his protégé of Caribbean origins, David 'Syd' Lawrence. Sections of the 10,000 crowd subjected the two of them to continuous racial abuse, chanting 'Sieg Heil', giving National Front salutes and hurling oranges and bananas onto the outfield. David Graveney, the Gloucestershire captain, said at the time that 'the root of what happened yesterday was drink' and that those carrying out the drunken abuse were not a mindless minority but ' ... much more than a minority'. Yorkshire County Cricket Club apologised formally and Shepherd, who said that he 'had played all over the world and had never met such aggression from a crowd before',[155] received dozens of letters of apology and support from across Yorkshire and beyond.

1985 and later

At the end of 1984 Gloucestershire offered John Shepherd a new three-year contract which was to involve him increasingly in coaching. It was financially a fairly generous offer with a basic salary of £7,500 and a further £4,000 for his 'coaching duties'. Gloucestershire had recognised that Shep was a natural coach - although at the time he had no formal coaching qualifications. His allround track record as a player - by then he had played in 421 first-class matches, 13,353 runs and 1,155 wickets - was unrivalled and he was also still one of the country's leading practitioners in the one-day game. He was an effective communicator, especially with young players with whom he had an easy rapport. The young fast bowler David Lawrence had been particularly under Shepherd's wing in 1984 and his progress had been marked.

In 1985 Shepherd played a handful of mostly one-day first-team games in the early season before concentrating on his coaching role - this included captaining the Second Eleven, a task he continued with in 1986 and 1987. He recalls that one of the reasons that he put a considerable effort into the seconds and the mostly young players in that squad was that he found the Gloucestershire captain David Graveney rather unwilling to have him performing a hands-on coaching role with the first-team players, even though Shep had been officially designated as 'Senior Coach' at the beginning of the year. The rather prickly Graveney jealously guarded his position of authority as club captain and Shepherd opted not to take him on.

The Shepherd family was now complete with the arrival of a son, David, in 1983 to join his sisters Caroline, born 1976, and Jacqueline, born 1978. The

155 *The Times*, 10 July 1984.

family had established themselves comfortably in a pleasant house in the Gloucestershire market town of Chipping Sodbury. The three-year contract offered John by the county allowed them at least to plan a few years ahead, although as he had found to his cost once before, there were no certainties in the world of cricket employment. Over the next few years he threw himself enthusiastically into his coaching task and there was to be an immediate payback for his work with Syd Lawrence who took 79 first-class wickets in 1985 and, together with the county's inspired overseas player signings of Courtney Walsh and Kevin Curran, helped the county to rise to third place in the County Championship. The club was evidently pleased with Shepherd's contribution as coach and extended his contract for a fourth year up to the end of the 1988 season.

Towards the end of the 1987 season Gloucestershire had 'enough injured players to keep a sports injuries clinic working full time'[156] and an emergency call went out to Shepherd, at the age of 43, to play in two Sunday League matches and one Championship game. In one of the Sunday games Shep helped Gloucestershire to beat Nottinghamshire, taking the wickets of Test players Tim Robinson and Clive Rice in the process. The Championship match, the last first-class match of John Shepherd's career, started on 9 September 1987, over twenty-two years since his first in February 1965, was at Grace Road, Leicester. Shepherd took two wickets in Leicestershire's first innings, Potter and DeFreitas, as well as catches to dismiss Peter Willey and David Gower. His final efforts with the bat were less distinguished - out for five in the first innings and bowled for one by Leslie Taylor in the second.

Whilst John Shepherd's professional cricket career continued to run smoothly through the 1980s, sadly at home things were beginning to be desperately difficult. Terry Shepherd had been suffering from ill health for some years and despite a series of tests doctors had failed to diagnose the cause of her problem. In 1987 John and Terry took the decision to move the family back to Kent where Terry could be closer to old friends and also to the Canterbury hospital where she had worked as a nurse for many years. They bought a house in Beltinge, a suburb of Herne Bay, on the north Kent coast. During the cricket season John made use of a small flat in Nevil Road, Bristol owned by the club - for a very close-knit family this was very disruptive but worse was to follow. In 1989 Shep had been offered a further two-year contract as Senior Coach, although they had turned down his request for a benefit or a testimonial which he thought he was due after seven years' service as player and coach. The club was, however, concerned that Shepherd's difficult personal circumstances would interfere with his ability fully to fulfil his role and asked for a commitment from him that he would be 'here in Bristol on a full-time basis in the summer and this includes weekends'.[157] In April 1989, just as the cricket season was

156 Geoffrey Wheeler, in *Wisden*, 1988.

157 Letter to John Shepherd from Gloucestershire CCC secretary, Philip August, on 17 January 1989.

beginning, a consultant finally diagnosed Terry Shepherd to be suffering from cancer of the lymph nodes. It was with this knowledge that Shep worked at Bristol, including captaining the Gloucestershire Second Eleven in two matches, the second of which, against Derbyshire on 10, 11 and 12 May, was to be his last ever senior cricket appearance.

Terry Shepherd died in July 1989. John and his three children, now aged 13, 11 and 6, had not only to cope with grief but also to try and find a practical way to live as a one-parent family. The younger daughter, the eleven-year-old Jacqueline, reassured her father: 'Don't you worry Dad, we'll look after you.' 'Oh dear' thought John, 'isn't that my line?' John's mother flew in from Barbados and was to stay for six months as John fulfilled his commitment to Gloucestershire, where it was mutually agreed that he would leave the county at the end of the 1989 season. There is never an ideal time for bereavement but for John to be widowed at this time, knowing that his longer-term employment at Gloucestershire was uncertain, and with no immediate prospects of alternative work and no pension or other income source, it was doubly hard. He had secured an interview at Sussex for their vacant coach's job but lost out to Norman Gifford. He had heard nothing from Kent County Cricket Club and a sense of pride stopped him from knocking on their door – convenient though it would have been to return to his original English cricket home.

Although the children were still young, John Shepherd was a competent house-husband – he knew how to cook and wash and clean, and in the year after his wife's death it was inevitably the children that were his first priority. But he knew that he must find a job and also that at the age of 46 this might be difficult. He trod water for a while, carrying out some talent spotting around the Kent schools on behalf of a wealthy businessman and cricket enthusiast John Martin, but this half-job finished at the end of 1991 and John then thought seriously about moving with the children back to Barbados. He gave an interview to the *Kent Messenger* to this effect and this led shortly to an approach from Graham Cowdrey as to whether Shep might be interested in a cricket professional vacancy at the independent school Eastbourne College. The Cowdrey family had good connections in Sussex, especially since Colin Cowdrey had established himself at Angmering Park, Littlehampton, in 1985 on his marriage to Lady Herries. An interview and job offer followed and in 1992 Shepherd took up the post of cricket professional at the school. As well as being a job for which he was ideally suited there were also attractive fringe benefits – a four-bedroomed flat was made available at a peppercorn rent and his children were admitted to the school at very advantageous fees. The cricket facilities at the school were excellent and the overall atmosphere was delightful – especially after the trauma of bereavement and the stressful world of county cricket. In his first year at the school, Shep guided the First Eleven to an unbeaten season which included wins over most of their main rivals and in 1993 the Cowdreys' *alma mater* Tonbridge was defeated. A star pupil was Alex Bogdanovski who had clearly inherited some of his cricketing prowess from his uncle, the England allrounder Phil Edmonds. Bogdanovski remembers[158] John Shepherd as being:

> ... always very passionate about cricket ... and I think he was always a little shocked how as schoolboys we took cricket as something we did from 3-5pm, a pastime, a bit of fun, it was always so much more to John ... he struggled to comprehend the ambivalence of the average school boy towards cricket. He loved it - why didn't we love it as much as he did? In one game ... I remember sticking John back over his own head for a big six into the road. I was a slightly chippy character back then, and I didn't have to work too hard to irritate many of the staff, most of whom would have been seething to have themselves despatched in this way. John on the other hand was just grinning at me! To him the incident was all about pride as a coach rather than any concern that it was his bowling that had been trounced.

Perhaps also John was remembering the sixteen-year-old who had hit the ball out of the ground at Belleplaine Cricket Club back in 1959 and for whom cricket then as now was one of the great joys of life.

John's time at Eastbourne was to be happy not only because he was in a job that he loved and which had come to him at an ideal time in his life, but also because he met a lady, Susan Davies, with whom he was to form a close attachment and to whom he would be married in December 1999. The 'father-giver' at the wedding was the man who had brought John Shepherd to England thirty-five years earlier - now Lord Cowdrey of Tonbridge.

John and Sue Shepherd at their wedding at Eastbourne College in December 1999.

158 E-mail to the author, December 2008.

Colin Cowdrey and John Shepherd at John's wedding in Eastbourne in 1999.

Cowdrey was frail and ill but was determined to be present and to deliver a warm and emotional speech at the wedding which was held in the beautiful chapel of Eastbourne College. There was nary a dry eye in the house! A year after Shep's wedding Cowdrey died at the age of 67, and in March 2001 Shep joined his colleagues from the 1970 Championship-winning team to walk together in tribute down the aisle of Westminster Abbey at Cowdrey's memorial service.

There is one last brief chapter in the 'third innings' of John Shepherd's 'Life in Cricket'. He spent two rather frustrating years working for the International Cricket Council as 'Regional Development Officer' for the Americas region, based at the West Indies Cricket Board (WICB) in Antigua. The job was ill-defined and included responsibility for the development of the game in both North and South America. The region was far too broadly scoped and the rivalries and organisational confusions that Shep stumbled into were huge and way beyond the capability of one man, however smart and cricket-savvy, to cope with. The WICB was at times a reluctant host and never a very hospitable one – even to one of their own. For John and Sue Shepherd, whilst there was much delight in living on a beautiful Caribbean island, there was great frustration that the job Shep was so earnestly trying to do was an impossible one.

In November 2003 John Shepherd celebrated his sixtieth birthday, back now, with Sue, in Kent in a lovely house in a quiet road in Herne Bay. This naturally-gifted sportsman now played golf off a low, single-figure handicap and was a key member of the County Cricketers' Golf Society, playing regularly with old colleagues such as Derek Underwood and Mike Denness. He had also carved a niche for himself as a regular accompanier of spectators on cricket tours – not the Barmy Army but rather quieter cricket followers whose shared ambition was to see England play around the world. And there we shall leave him: captain of Herne Bay Golf Club, cricket legend, devoted father and loving husband.

The Belleplaine Boy has come a very long way indeed.

John Shepherd, at home in Herne Bay in January 2009, with a portrait given to him during his Kent benefit year, 1979.

Acknowledgements

John Shepherd gave unstintingly of his time and without him this book would not have been possible. I am indebted to him and also to his wife Sue for their patience, kindness and hospitality.

In *Barbados,* Mac D Smith showed me around St Andrew and John Shepherd's birthplace of Belleplaine. Sir Everton Weekes talked to me at length about John as a schoolboy and club cricketer and about the prelude to Shep's move to Kent in 1965 - I am immensely grateful to him for this and also for contributing the book's foreword. Tony Cozier spoke to me about John's Test career and about the implication in Barbados of his decision to play in Southern Africa. The C.L.R.James Cricket Research Centre Library at the University of the West Indies, in Cave Hill, was a useful source of reference.

Kent County Cricket Club gave me access to Committee minutes and other documents and records and I am grateful to David Robertson for his help and advice. Many ex-cricketers spoke to me about John and I am particularly grateful to Derek Underwood and Mike Denness for allowing me to spend some time with them to tap their memories of Shep's contribution to Kent's glory years.

In *South Africa,* Prof Andre Odendaal, now CEO of Western Province Cricket Association, spoke to me about John's Southern Africa time and read and commented helpfully on a draft of Chapter Five of the book.

The *ACS* has been supportive from the start – the editor David Jeater has been patient and helpful to a tyro biographer and Douglas Miller has been encouraging at all times and a wise counsel. I am grateful to them; to Peter Griffiths for the typesetting and his other contributions to the production process; to Philip Bailey for his statistical eagle eye; to Ric Finlay for help with John's statistics while playing for Footscray; to Gerald Hudd for his proofreading; and to Roger Mann for contributing photographs from his collection. The MCC library and its staff have been a great help where my own books failed me.

An early draft of the manuscript was read carefully by my wife Ann and by my good friends Nigel Lynch and David Marshall, all of whom corrected countless grammatical, punctuation and other errors which saved me embarrassment when I submitted a revised version to the editor.

Paddy Briggs
Teddington
April, 2009

Bibliography

Key reference sources were *Wisden Cricketers' Almanack, Playfair Cricket Annual*, the *Kent County Cricket Annual*, the *Gloucestershire County Cricket Club Year Book, The Cricketer magazine*, and various *Wisden* anthologies.

Other books consulted, and sometimes quoted from, include:

Allen, David Rayvern, *Arlott*, Harper Collins, 1994

Allen, David Rayvern, *Jim: The Life of E.W.Swanton*, Aurum Press, 2004

Arrowsmith, R.L., *A History of County Cricket: Kent*, Sportsmans Book Club, 1972

Bailey, Trevor, *The Greatest of My Time*, Eyre and Spottiswoode, 1968

Bailey, Trevor (ed), *World of Cricket Annual 1978*, Macdonald and Jane's Publishers, 1978

Barrett, Norman, *The Daily Telegraph Chronicle of Cricket*, Guinness Publishing, 1994

Beckles, Hilary McD., *A Spirit of Dominance*, University of West Indies Press, 1998

Beckles, Hilary McD., *The Development of West Indies Cricket, Volumes 1 and 2*, Pluto Press, both 1998

Black, Bernard, *Colin Cowdrey in Test Cricket*, published by its author, 2005

Brooke, Robert, *A History of County Championship Cricket*, Guinness Publishing, 1991

Buckland, William, *Pommies: England Cricket Through an Australian Lens*, Matador, 2008

Close, Brian (with Don Mosey), *I Don't Bruise Easily*, Macdonald and Jane's Publishers, 1978

Constantine, Learie, *Colour Bar*, Stanley Paul, 1954

Cowdrey, Colin, *Time for Reflection*, Sportsmans Book Club, 1963

Cowdrey, Colin, *MCC: The Autobiography of a Cricketer*, Hodder and Stoughton, 1976

Cowdrey, Colin, *Cricket Today*, Arthur Barker, 1961

Cox, Peter, *Sixty Summers: English Cricket Since World War 2*, Labatie Books, 2006

Denness, Mike, *I Declare*, Arthur Barker, 1977

Evans, John (with Derek Carlaw and Howard Milton), *Images of Kent Cricket*, Breedon Books, 2000

Fowle, Dennis, *Kent: The Glory Years*, Everest Books, 1974

Bill Frindall (ed), *The Wisden Book of Test Cricket, Volumes 1 and 2*, Headline, 1984 and 2000

Goble, Ray and Keith A.P.Sandiford, *75 Years of West Indies Cricket*, Hansib, 2004

Goodwin, Clayton, *Caribbean Cricketers*, Harrap, 1980

Green, Stephen, Lord's: *The Cathedral of Cricket*, Tempus, 2003

Green, David, *The History of the Gloucestershire County Cricket Club*, Christopher Helm, 1990

Hain, Peter, *Don't Play With Apartheid*, George Allen and Unwin, 1971

Hartland, Peter, *The Balance of Power in Test Cricket*, Field Publishing, 1998

Hayes, Dean, *Kent County Cricket Club, An A to Z*, SB Publications, 2002

Heffer, Simon (ed), *The Daily Telegraph Century of County Cricket*, Sidgwick and Jackson, 1990

Hill, Alan, *Les Ames*, Christopher Helm, 1990

Hunte, Conrad, *Playing To Win*, Hodder and Stoughton, 1971

Hussain, Nasser, *Playing With Fire*, Michael Joseph, 2004

Illingworth, Ray (with Don Mosey), *Yorkshire and Back*, Queen Anne Press, 1980

James, C.L.R., *A Majestic Innings*, Aurum Press, 2006

James, C.L.R., *Beyond A Boundary* (Revised Edition), Yellow Jersey Press, 2005

Knott, Alan, *It's Knott Cricket*, Macmillan, 1985

Luckhurst, Brian (as told to Mark Baldwin), *Boot Boy to President*, KOS Media, 2004

Major, John, *More Than A Game*, Harper Press , 2007

Manley, Michael (with Donna Symonds), *A History of West Indies Cricket*, André Deutsch, 1988

Martin-Jenkins, Christopher, *The Spirit of Cricket*, Faber and Faber, 1994

Martin-Jenkins, Christopher, *Twenty Years On*, Willow Books, 1984

Milton, Howard, *Lord Cowdrey of Tonbridge*, ACS Publications (Famous Cricketers Series), 2003

Moore, Dudley, *The History of Kent County Cricket Club*, Christopher Helm, 1988

Mortimer, David, *Classic Cricket Clangers*, Robson Books, 2003

Oborne, Peter, *Basil D'Oliveira: Cricket and Conspiracy*, Little, Brown, 2004

Odendaal, André, *Cricket in Isolation*, published by its author, 1977

Odendaal, André, *The Story of an African Game*, David Philip, 2003

Peel, Mark, *The Last Roman*, André Deutsch, 1999

Powell, William, *Images of Sport: Kent County Cricket Club*, Tempus, 2000

Puxley, J.H. (ed), *John Shepherd Benefit Souvenir*, Kent County Cricket Club, 1979

Rice, Jonathan, *One Hundred Lord's Tests*, Methuen, 2001

Richards, Jimmy, *Statistics of West Indies Cricket: 1865–1989*, Heinemann, 2001

Robertson, David, *Kent County Cricket Club: 100 Greats*, Tempus, 2005

Robertson, David, Howard Milton and Derek Carlaw, *Kent County Cricket Club, 100 Greats*, Tempus, 2005

Robertson, David, Howard Milton and Derek Carlaw, *Kent County Cricket Club, Fifty of the Finest First-Class Matches*, Tempus, 2006

Sandiford, Keith A.P., *Cricket Nurseries of Colonial Barbados*, University of West Indies Press, 1998

Sandiford, Keith A.P. (ed), *100 Years of Organised Cricket in Barbados: 1892–1992*, Barbados Cricket Association, 1992

Sobers, Garry, *My Autobiography*, Headline, 2002

Sobers, Sir Garfield, *Twenty Years At The Top*, Macmillan, 1988

Stout, Deborah (ed), *The 3Ws: A Legacy of West Indian Cricket*, The 3Ws Committee, 2003

Swanton, E.W., *Back Page Cricket*, Queen Anne Press, 1987

Swanton, E.W. and C.H.Taylor, *Kent Cricket: A Photographic History*, Geerings of Ashford, 1988

Tennant, Ivo, *The Cowdreys: Portrait of a Cricketing Family*, Simon and Schuster, 1990

Underwood, Derek, *Beating the Bat*, Stanley Paul, 1975

Underwood, Derek, *Deadly Down Under*, Arthur Barker, 1980

Walcott, Clyde (with Brian Scovell), *Sixty Years on the Back Foot*, Victor Gollancz, 1999

Max Walker, *How to Hypnotise Chooks*, Gary Sparke, 1987

Ward, Andrew, *Cricket's Strangest Matches*, Robson Books, 1999

Weekes, Sir Everton (with Hilary McD.Beckles), *Mastering the Craft*, Universities of the Caribbean Press, 2007

Williams, Jack, *Cricket and Race*, Berg, 2001

Willis, Bob (with Patrick Murphy), *The Cricket Revolution*, Sidgwick and Jackson, 1981

Woods, John, *Test Cricket Grounds*, SportsBooks, 2004

Woolmer, Bob, *Pirate and Rebel?*, Arthur Barker, 1984

The principal contemporary newspaper match reports consulted were in *The Times*, *The Daily Telegraph* and *The Guardian.*

Online sources include www.cricketarchive.com and www.cricinfo.com

Appendix

Career Statistics

Test cricket: Batting and Fielding

		M	*I*	*NO*	*R*	*HS*	*Ave*	*100*	*50*	*Ct*
1969	England	3	5	0	65	32	13.00	-	-	1
1970/71	West Indies	2	3	0	12	9	4.00	-	-	3
Total		**5**	**8**	**0**	**77**	**32**	**9.62**	**-**	**-**	**4**

Test cricket: Bowling

		O	*M*	*R*	*W*	*BB*	*Ave*	*5i*
1969	England	137.5	44	266	12	5-104	22.16	1
1970/71	WI	103	26	213	7	3-78	30.42	-
Total		**240.5**	**70**	**479**	**19**	**5-104**	**25.21**	**1**

First-class cicket: Batting and Fielding

		M	*I*	*NO*	*R*	*HS*	*Ave*	*100*	*50*	*Ct*
1964/65	West Indies	1	2	0	55	33	27.50	-	-	-
1966	England	1	1	0	17	17	17.00	-	-	-
1967	England	29	41	6	951	73*	27.17	-	7	37
1967/68	West Indies	1	2	0	10	6	5.00	-	-	-
1968	England	28	42	3	1157	170	29.66	3	7	27
1968/69	West Indies	4	7	0	186	73	26.57	-	1	6
1969	England	17	22	4	255	32	14.16	-	-	8
1970	England	25	36	4	734	105	22.93	1	2	23
1970/71	West Indies	6	9	1	118	68*	14.75	-	1	9
1971	England	26	40	5	792	81	22.62	-	5	26
1972	England	20	27	7	333	51	16.65	-	1	9
1973	England	24	35	4	803	87	25.90	-	5	11
1973/74	South Africa	7	7	0	169	53	24.14	-	1	4
1974	England	21	30	6	609	79	25.37	-	2	6
1974/75	South Africa	7	12	5	397	71*	56.71	-	3	5
1975	England	19	30	7	735	116	31.95	1	3	9
1975/76	South Africa	9	16	1	298	65	19.86	-	2	6
1976	England	16	29	6	895	87	38.91	-	8	11
1977	England	20	25	4	446	77	21.23	-	2	18
1978	England	20	28	6	785	101	35.68	2	3	12
1979	England	16	20	1	370	86	19.47	-	1	9
1980	England	20	23	8	428	100	28.53	1	1	8
1981	England	15	20	6	310	59*	22.14	-	2	4
1982	England	22	34	9	590	67*	23.60	-	3	13
1983	England	23	34	6	1025	168	36.60	2	6	16
1984	England	24	39	7	885	87	27.65	-	6	13
1985	England	1	0					-	-	-
1987	England	1	2	0	6	5	3.00	-	-	2
Totals		**423**	**613**	**106**	**13359**	**170**	**26.34**	**10**	**72**	**292**

Notes: Shepherd was dismissed 306 times caught (60%), including 59 times by identified wicket-keepers; 108 times bowled (21%); 74 times lbw (15%), 15 times run out (3%) and four times stumped. He was dismissed most often by Intikhab Alam 8, by P.I.Pocock 7 and by W.W.Daniel, R.E.East, N.Gifford, K.Higgs, J.A.Snow and P.Willey, all 6. The bowler from whom he took most catches was D.L.Underwood, with 59; 40 of his catches were off his own bowling.

First-class cricket: Bowling

		O	*M*	*R*	*W*	*BB*	*Ave*	*5i*	*10m*
1964/65	WI	33	3	111	2	1-54	55.50	-	-
1966	Eng	37	11	85	5	4-71	17.00	-	-
1967	Eng	568.3	182	1113	54	7-85	20.61	4	-
1967/68	WI	27	9	87	0	-	-	-	-
1968	Eng	752.2	238	1798	96	6-60	18.72	8	-
1968/69	WI	90.2	28	202	7	2-10	28.85	-	-
1969	Eng	384.3	114	930	31	8-40	30.00	2	-
1970	Eng	894.5	231	2320	86	6-33	26.97	6	-
1970/71	WI	178	45	405	17	4-40	23.82	-	-
1971	Eng	768.5	199	1946	59	6-36	32.98	2	-
1972	Eng	591.4	155	1469	48	7-38	30.60	2	-
1973	Eng	800.3	229	2054	92	6-127	22.32	7	1
1973/74	SA	208	45	566	15	4-54	37.73	-	-
1974	Eng	641	154	1691	55	6-42	30.74	2	-
1974/75	SA	219.3	41	648	23	4-37	28.17	-	-
1975	Eng	579.2	146	1465	52	8-93	28.17	3	1
1975/76	SA	266.5	62	662	26	3-34	25.46	-	-
1976	Eng	496.2	106	1347	48	5-69	28.06	2	-
1977	Eng	738.4	216	1734	87	8-83	19.93	6	-
1978	Eng	601.2	166	1573	44	5-70	35.75	1	-
1979	Eng	418.3	114	1075	34	4-55	31.61	-	-
1980	Eng	473.1	118	1220	44	5-40	27.72	1	-
1981	Eng	424.3	111	1136	28	5-61	40.57	1	-
1982	Eng	742.1	177	2026	63	6-75	32.15	2	-
1983	Eng	776.1	209	2047	67	7-50	30.55	3	-
1984	Eng	800.3	209	2225	72	5-30	30.90	2	-
1985	Eng	14	3	41	0	-	-	-	-
1987	Eng	28	9	92	2	2-42	46.00	-	-
Totals		**12554.3**	**3330**	**32068**	**1157**	**8-40**	**27.71**	**54**	**2**

Notes: Overs were of six balls throughout Shepherd's first-class career. He took his wickets at the rate of one per 65.10 balls and conceded runs at the rate of 2.55 per over. Of his 1,157 wickets, 762 (66%) were caught; 244 (21%) were bowled; 150 (13%) were lbw and one hit wicket. Of those caught, 365 – 32 % of all his wickets, an exceptional proportion – were taken by identified wicketkeepers. None were stumped. He dismissed three batsmen ten or more times; these were B.A.Richards 13, C.T.Radley 12 and J.M.Brearley 10.

First-class cricket: Centuries (10)

Score	For	Opponent	Venue	Season
106*	Kent[2]	Hampshire	Southampton	1968
103	Kent[2]	Middlesex	Lord's	1968
170	Kent[1]	Northamptonshire	Folkestone	1968
105	Kent[1]	Hampshire	Portsmouth	1970
116	Kent[2]	Middlesex	Canterbury	1975
101	Kent[1]	Surrey	Tunbridge Wells	1978
100*	Kent[1]	Worcestershire	Worcester	1978

100	Kent[1]	Surrey	Maidstone	1980
168	Gloucestershire[2]	Warwickshire	Edgbaston	1983
112	Gloucestershire[1]	Kent	Bristol	1983

Shepherd also reached 98 and then ran out of partners, for Gloucestershire v Glamorgan at Cheltenham in 1983.*

First-Class cricket: Five wickets or more in an innings (54)

Bowling	For	Opponent	Venue	Season
43-11-85-7	Kent	Middlesex[1]	Blackheath	1967
24-5-59-5	Kent	Essex[1]	Leyton	1967
49-17-71-6	Kent	Derbyshire[1]	Burton-on-Trent	1967
18-7-34-5	Kent	Warwickshire[1]	Dover	1967
12.4-3-22-5	Kent	Cambridge Univ[1]	Fenner's	1968
17-3-49-5	Kent	Surrey[1]	Blackheath	1968
14-5-28-5	Kent	Lancashire[1]	Old Trafford	1968
21-4-45-5	Kent	Glamorgan[2]	Swansea	1968
23-8-63-5	Kent	Somerset[2]	Weston-super-Mare	1968
38.5-21-60-6	Kent	Warwickshire[1]	Canterbury	1968
26.5-11-34-5	Kent	Northamptonshire[2]	Wellingborough	1968
12-4-30-5	Kent	Glamorgan[1]	Folkestone	1968
21.3-7-40-8	West Indians	Gloucestershire[1]	Bristol	1969
58.5-19-105-5	WEST INDIES	ENGLAND[1]	OLD TRAFFORD	1969
29-5-89-6	Kent	Leicestershire[2]	Leicester	1970
19.5-6-41-5	Kent	Essex[1]	Harlow	1970
52-10-123-5	Kent	Yorkshire[1]	Sheffield (Bramall)	1970
25.3-11-45-5	Kent	Sussex[1]	Hove	1970
18-6-33-6	Kent	Middlesex[1]	Canterbury	1970
20-7-64-5	Kent	Leicestershire[1]	Folkestone	1970
20.5-7-36-6	Kent	Yorkshire[2]	Bradford	1971
35-16-60-5	Kent	Lancashire[2]	Southport	1971
21.4-3-38-7	Kent	Gloucestershire[1]	Tunbridge Wells	1972
24.5-15-24-5	Kent	Worcestershire[2]	Worcester	1972
27-5-72-5	Kent	MCC[1]	Canterbury	1973
26-7-67-5	Kent	Middlesex[1]	Lord's	1973
33.3-4-127-6	Kent	Middlesex[1]	Dover	1973
30-12-58-5	Kent	Yorkshire[1]	Canterbury	1973
25.3-1-92-5	Kent	Essex[1]	Leyton	1973
35-15-80-5	Kent	Leicestershire[1]	Folkestone	1973
26-6-81-5	Kent	Leicestershire[2]	Folkestone	1973
25-8-42-6	Kent	Glamorgan[1]	Maidstone	1974
33-11-67-6	Kent	Warwickshire[1]	Canterbury	1974
32.5-6-93-8	Kent	Sussex[1]	Maidstone	1975
29-11-54-7	Kent	Sussex[2]	Maidstone	1975
24-10-59-5	Kent	Lancashire[2]	Tunbridge Wells	1975
19-0-69-5	Kent	Hampshire[2]	Maidstone	1976
36-5-113-5	Kent	Somerset[1]	Taunton	1976
10.4-2-25-5	Kent	Gloucestershire[2]	Bristol	1977
23-11-33-5	Kent	Middlesex[1]	Dartford	1977
37-12-83-8	Kent	Lancashire[1]	Tunbridge Wells	1977
25-10-38-5	Kent	Worcestershire[1]	Canterbury	1977
23-5-58-5	Kent	Nottinghamshire[1]	Canterbury	1977
20.1-6-63-5	Kent	Warwickshire[1]	Edgbaston	1977
24-8-70-5	Kent	Somerset[1]	Taunton	1978
19.2-7-40-5	Kent	Yorkshire[1]	Sheffield (Abbeydale)	1980
31-12-61-5	Kent	Middlesex[1]	Lord's	1981
33.1-5-75-6	Gloucestershire	Sussex[1]	Hastings	1982
14.3-2-43-5	Gloucestershire	Yorkshire[2]	Bradford	1982

28-12-50-7	Gloucestershire	Warwickshire[1]	Edgbaston	1983
27-7-80-5	Gloucestershire	Somerset[1]	Bath	1983
32-10-64-7	Gloucestershire	Glamorgan[2]	Cheltenham	1983
21.4-6-30-5	Gloucestershire	Kent[2]	Canterbury	1984
32-7-116-5	Gloucestershire	Warwickshire[1]	Edgbaston	1984

Note: The index figures [1] and [2] in this and the preceding table indicate the innings in which the feat was achieved.

List A limited-overs cricket: Batting and Fielding

		M	*I*	*NO*	*R*	*HS*	*Ave*	*100*	*50*	*Ct*
1967	England	5	4	0	118	77	29.50	-	1	2
1968	England	1	1	0	0	0	0.00	-	-	-
1969	England	5	5	1	32	20	8.00	-	-	-
1970	England	18	16	3	260	40	20.00	-	-	4
1971	England	21	19	3	460	65	28.75	-	3	7
1972	England	24	17	4	160	28*	12.30	-	-	8
1973	England	21	16	4	237	39	19.75	-	-	7
1974	England	25	21	8	285	28	21.92	-	-	5
1974/75	South Africa	3	3	0	87	48	29.00	-	-	-
1975	England	19	14	2	246	96	20.50	-	1	7
1975/76	South Africa	2	2	1	11	8	11.00	-	-	1
1976	England	21	19	4	460	58	30.66	-	2	3
1977	England	17	16	1	320	101	21.33	1	1	3
1978	England	21	18	4	380	94	27.14	-	2	10
1979	England	19	17	4	362	63	27.84	-	2	7
1980	England	16	12	6	101	28*	16.83	-	-	7
1981	England	18	12	0	141	22	11.75	-	-	4
1982	England	19	15	4	253	47	23.00	-	-	5
1983	England	20	16	6	196	35	19.60	-	-	2
1984	England	18	16	3	199	52*	15.30	-	1	3
1985	England	11	6	2	28	11*	7.00	-	-	1
1986	England	2	1	0	1	1	1.00	-	-	-
Total		**326**	**266**	**60**	**4337**	**101**	**21.05**	**1**	**13**	**86**

Notes: The figures for the 'England' season of 1983 include the Benson and Hedges Cup match Scotland v Gloucestershire, played in Glasgow on 17 May. Of his 206 dismissals, Shepherd was caught 113 times (55%); bowled 64 times (31%); lbw 17 times (6%); run out 11 times (5%) and stumped once. Three bowlers dismissed him more than three times, C.H.Dredge, A.W.Greig and J.F.Steele all with four. The bowler from whom he took most catches was D.L.Underwood, with 19; 17 of his catches were off his own bowling.

List A limited overs cricket: Bowling

		O	*M*	*R*	*W*	*BB*	*Ave*	*4i*
1967	Eng	44	9	132	3	2-27	44.00	-
1968	Eng	12	6	16	2	2-16	8.00	-
1969	Eng	34	8	85	4	3-19	21.25	-
1970	Eng	132	9	537	25	3-20	21.48	-
1971	Eng	175.5	21	601	37	4-20	16.24	3
1972	Eng	202	21	690	37	4-18	18.64	2
1973	Eng	172.3	21	639	24	4-43	26.62	1
1974	Eng	210.3	23	718	34	3-23	21.11	-
1974/75	SA	26	8	71	5	2-20	14.20	-
1975	Eng	149.4	20	557	29	3-15	19.20	-
1975/76	SA	21	4	66	0	-	-	-

1976	Eng	169	18	602	24	4-30	25.08	1
1977	Eng	116.1	7	427	13	2-23	32.84	-
1978	Eng	157.3	25	473	34	4-17	13.91	3
1979	Eng	143.1	24	436	27	4-32	16.14	1
1980	Eng	109.1	10	425	20	3-26	21.25	-
1981	Eng	128.1	15	442	19	3-24	23.26	-
1982	Eng	166	13	734	26	3-16	28.23	-
1983	Eng	155.4	11	668	36	6-52	18.55	1
1984	Eng	161.4	14	659	25	4-20	26.36	2
1985	Eng	82	4	391	10	2-42	39.10	-
1987	Eng	12	1	60	2	2-20	30.00	-
Totals		**2580**	**292**	**9429**	**436**	**6-52**	**21.62**	**14**

Notes: Overs were of six balls throughout Shepherd's limited-overs career. The figures for the 'England' season of 1983 include the Benson and Hedges Cup match Scotland v Gloucestershire, played in Glasgow on 17 May. He took his wickets at the rate of one per 35.50 balls and conceded runs at the rate of 3.65 per over. Of his 436 wickets, 290 (67%) were caught; 110 (25%) were bowled; 33 (8%) were lbw, two were stumped and one hit wicket. He dismissed S.Turner seven times; no other batsman more than five times.

List A limited-overs cricket: Fifties (14)

Score	For	Opponent	Venue	Season
77	Kent	Sussex	Canterbury	1967
52*	Kent	Northamptonshire	Northampton	1971
65	Kent	Surrey	The Oval	1971
53	Kent	Middlesex	Canterbury	1971
96	Kent	Middlesex	Lord's	1975
58	Kent	Derbyshire	Folkestone	1976
51*	Kent	Lancashire	Old Trafford	1976
101	Kent	Middlesex	Canterbury	1977
55	Kent	Gloucestershire	Lord's	1977
52*	Kent	Warwickshire	Edgbaston	1978
94	Kent	Hampshire	Southampton	1978
63	Kent	Gloucestershire	Gloucester (Tuffley)	1979
55*	Kent	Lancashire	Maidstone	1979
52*	Gloucestershire	Nottinghamshire	Trent Bridge	1984

Notes: Shepherd's 55 against Gloucestershire in 1977 was in the Benson and Hedges Cup final.

List A limited-overs cricket: Four wickets or more in an innings (14)

Bowling	For	Opponent	Venue	Season
10.2-0-26-4	Kent	Yorkshire	Canterbury	1971
8-2-20-4	Kent	Somerset	Canterbury	1971
8-1-27-4	Kent	Hampshire	Maidstone	1971
8-0-18-4	Kent	Hampshire	Portsmouth	1972
12-5-23-4	Kent	Essex	Leyton	1972
12-3-43-4	Kent	Hampshire	Canterbury	1973
6-0-30-4	Kent	Nottinghamshire	Trent Bridge	1976
6.2-0-17-4	Kent	Middlesex	Lord's	1978
12-1-38-4	Kent	Northamptonshire	Northampton	1978
11-2-25-4	Kent	Derbyshire	Lord's	1978
11-4-32-4	Kent	Middlesex	Canterbury	1979
8-0-52-6	Gloucestershire	Kent	Bristol	1983

8-0-33-4	Gloucestershire	Nottinghamshire	Trent Bridge	1984
12-3-20-4	Gloucestershire	Staffordshire	Stone	1984

Note: Shepherd's 4-25 against Derbyshire in 1978 was in the Benson and Hedges Cup final.

Senior cricket: Batting, Bowling and Fielding

The table below summarises Shepherd's appearances in 'senior' cricket. The matches covered include all his first-class and List A limited-overs matches; International Cavaliers matches in England from 1965 to 1970; Fenner and Tilcon Trophy matches in 1973, 1980 and 1982; World Cup 'warm-up' matches in 1975 and 1979; County Second Eleven championship matches and limited-overs matches for Kent in 1965 to 1970 and for Gloucestershire in 1985 to 1989; matches on Gloucestershire's tour of Sri Lanka in 1986/87, and for Footscray in Melbourne grade cricket in 1976/77 and 1977/78.

			Batting		**Bowling**		
		M	***R***	***Ave***	***Wkt***	***Ave***	***Ct/St***
1964/65	West Indies	1	55	27.50	2	55.50	-
1965	England	21	745	28.65	35	26.34	17/1
1966	England	27	937	31.23	65	19.75	28
1967	England	36	1084	26.43	57	22.80	41
1967/68	West Indies	2	36	18.00	1	139.00	1
1968	England	31	1290	30.00	98	19.34	27
1968/69	West Indies	4	186	26.57	7	28.85	6
1969	England	23	287	13.04	38	26.71	9
1970	England	44	1046	22.73	112	25.97	27
1970/71	West Indies	6	118	14.75	17	23.82	9
1971	England	49	1272	24.00	99	22.68	34
1972	England	46	620	18.23	88	26.85	17
1973	England	47	1082	24.04	122	22.54	19
1973/74	South Africa	7	169	24.14	15	37.73	4
1974	England	48	950	24.35	91	27.05	13
1974/75	South Africa	11	485	44.09	30	24.86	5
1975	England	41	1129	30.51	83	24.93	16
1975/76	South Africa	14	394	20.73	26	28.19	7
1976	England	38	1410	36.15	72	27.80	14
1976/77	Australia	10	458	38.17	32	14.34	4
1977	England	37	766	21.27	100	21.61	21
1977/78	Australia	11	449	37.42	48	10.56	5
1978	England	41	1165	32.36	78	26.23	22
1979	England	37	765	23.18	63	24.79	16
1980	England	38	551	25.04	64	26.00	15
1981	England	33	451	17.34	47	33.57	8
1982	England	43	857	22.55	92	30.32	18
1983	England	44	1221	32.13	103	26.54	18
1984	England	44	1156	24.50	97	30.15	16
1985	England	20	164	12.61	17	34.29	8
1986	England	10	260	37.14	10	28.80	9
1986/87	Sri Lanka	7	4	4.00	2	58.50	1
1987	England	16	210	17.50	21	25.47	10
1989	England	2	32	16.00	-	-	1
Totals		**889**	**21804**	**25.74**	**1832**	**25.35**	**466/1**

Notes: The figures for the 'England' season of 1983 include the Benson and Hedges Cup match Scotland v Gloucestershire, played in Glasgow on 17 May, and those for the 'England' season of 1969, the famous one-day match Ireland v West Indies at Sion Mills on 2 July. Shepherd's only stumping was in the Second Eleven Championship match Kent v Middlesex at Hesketh Park, Dartford on 9 and 10 August 1965, when he dismissed J.Butterfield off the bowling of G.W.Johnson.

Sources for all tables in this appendix: Wisden Cricketers' Almanack and cricketarchive.com

Index

A page number in bold indicates an illustration.